Broken Man Rebuilt by GOD

A JOURNAL ABOUT LOVE

LeRon Robinson

ISBN 979-8-88943-747-5 (paperback)
ISBN 979-8-88943-749-9 (digital)

Christian Faith Publishing
832 Park Avenue
Meadville, PA 16335
www.christianfaithpublishing.com

Printed in the United States of America

Love described in 1 Corinthians 13:1–13 (NIV):

If I speak in the tongues of men or of angels, but do not have love, I am only a resounding gong or a clanging cymbal. If I have the gift of prophecy and can fathom all mysteries and all knowledge, and if I have a faith that can move mountains, but do not have love, I am nothing. If I give all I possess to the poor and give over my body to hardship that I may boast, but do not have love, I gain nothing. Love is patient, love is kind. It does not envy, it does not boast, it is not proud. It does not dishonor others, it is not self-seeking, it is not easily angered, it keeps no record of wrongs. Love does not delight in evil but rejoices with the truth. It always protects, always trusts, always hopes, always perseveres. Love never fails. But where there are prophecies, they will cease; where there are tongues, they will be stilled; where there is knowledge, it will pass away. For we know in part and we prophesy in part, but when completeness comes, what is in part disappears. When I was a child, I talked like a child, I thought like a child, I reasoned like a child. When I became a man, I put the ways of childhood behind me. For now we see only a reflection as in a mirror; then we shall see face to face. Now I know in part; then I shall know fully, even as I am fully known. And now these three remain: faith, hope and love. But the greatest of these is love.

Someone to Wash My Back

A Short Journal from the Hand of a Broken Man in Search of God

In October 24, 2022, I was told I must write, so I did.

I have always had a unique personal struggle with understanding the many values inclusive with the word *love*, more important its true meaning. I longed to know how it distinctively pertained specifically to my life in all its forms. More often so, I think about my past and how love has molded me into a version of a man I do not believe I currently know. At my lowest, I allow my thoughts to drift. I go far back into life, deep into my dark history to a point where I end up dwelling on things which eventually send me spiraling into a severe state of depression.

My range of thoughts reflect on my many missed steps and corners cut. Generally, I come to an overwhelming consensus that my lack of love is a reflection of my upbringing, ignorance, and an unfortunate life filled with obstacles I never addressed. I begin to visually piece my own self sabotage together, recognizing my numerous faults, psychoanalyzing myself as if I graduated top of my class with the proper credentials to assess the mess.

This is typically followed by long periods of emotional stress and a stretch of regret where I find my flesh sitting in sorrow about an unclear tomorrow while constantly looping my history. Glaring into the sky aimlessly, I dwell on my mistakes and life choices which usually lead me into a darker place, left to ponder on all the what, when, where, how, and whys in my constant poor decision-making.

It is in this mode that I now have to deal with the real issues that have led me to my current emotional state without blaming anyone else as a cover-up or Band-Aid like most manipulators do.

These are the moments where most of us, me inclusive, find a space to speak with God. Usually when you have thought of it all, exhausted your means, and have nothing left to give. Yes, those of us who do not have the proper relationship with God, we get pushed here and then cry out aloud, "Dear God, if you hear me!"

God, why is this happening to me, not only now but in this manner? What have I done to deserve this? It's here with a face full of snot and tears I find myself looking for answers from the One. The One who, in all actuality, I should have been walking and talking with daily about all I was wrapped up in. More specifically, so that I could've come to a proper resolution, led to avoid my blow-ups and letdowns throughout life.

It's in my deepest moments of despair when I am reminded that I walk in sin. In between my own flaws and imperfection, I visualize a world full of sinners, and yet how is it I was itemized and placed in these conditions emotionally wrecked.

What made this the opportune moment to correct my actions or place me in time-out? I am not a murderer or a killer, I scream, as to hope for some sort of supernatural sympathy for my situation. I look at where I am, extremely confused about how I arrived here and all that has transpired. This isn't who I am, nor who I expected I would be; this isn't the dream sheet of tomorrow, my blueprint, or my list of what I needed to accomplish before leaving this earth.

I grow angrier wondering, is this repayment, even after all that I personally felt that I sacrificed? I contemplate my death in all forms and fashions only to be reminded that suicide is cowardly.

I am alone, and the silence is killer as my thoughts become weapons of mass destruction. Each log-on is a reminder of death and how life is not given enough attention to simply live it out to its fullest. The daily online and on-screen stories of individuals who have left without completing their God-given assignments because of the noise.

I believe that we are here for a specific life journey and reason. That ultimate decision is one we are not in full control over but how we maneuver the twist and turns en route to that place, for written our story to plateau is of our own footsteps. I believe that I am a child of God; I am to fail to learn, less not be judged because my flesh is not tainted; I'm truly flawed. It's my poor decisions, lack of spiritual consistency, and weakened mindset that have led me to places which allow for the devil to play and roam freely in my spirit.

This often results in the same pain replaying itself repeatedly. In my case, it was the norm when it revolved around love and my lack thereof. I guess you can say I was a gluten for its punishment or simply crazy. I allowed the evil to create a playground in my way of thinking over many years. There are many attributes I acquired to be a successful man, all of which I think run deep inside my being. There is also a dark corner reserved for the scared little boy I once was. He is the child that didn't get help. He was never seen nor heard. His voice is that of an echo and plays into the reason I now stand tall and yell inside rooms. He is the inner me, a sign of lost and lack, for he had many mistakes to answer for.

He goes unnoticed and is reserved because he could never be enough. The things he had to endure and overcome speak to his strength, a strength that goes unseen because his story goes untold. He has bruises and many scars, all before eighteen years of age. He lived his life backward taking on the role of a father and victim all in the same breath. He fights to maintain his sanity yet untreated is his pain.

It's this unique mixture of the two that get intertwined at times. They are separate yet one and complete me as a person. I would not be who I awaken to be without the little boy that once was. He is not the excuse for the ugliness I would eventually find myself in, yet he is large enough of a piece of the puzzle that his inclusion was needed in the picture.

After the shift in emotions, I am pushed to an intense state of solitude where I am left wondering if I am capable of utilizing any of my life skills, let alone the basic concepts which surround love and its use properly while feeling its lack so strong in my being on a day-in and day-out basis.

Time passes, and another shift is here. What you assume has been days has only been hours. It hurts; it digs into you. Morning has flashed its face, afternoon is now an afterthought, and it's night once again. It's the crucial moment after the tears get shed and the noise of your thoughts so slightly begin to return.

Once again, I am reminded that I have exhausted all of the earthly means I assumed I had. I break down; I look deep inside. Here is where I hear His voice call out, and I am reminded to find my faith.

It is here that I pray and hope that this little light can ever shine so bright again; it only flickers in its current state. I affirm to myself often in mantra form that "you have worth" and in my Kevin Garnett voice as it pertains to love and life, "Anything is possible!" Understanding that this only works if it is to be, more importantly, when you have God in your life properly and believe he is on your side.

The belief you have a major link securing your chain through-out your struggles. My path already scripted by the Creator. I gasp at my ever so unforeseen future. It is vague in photographic state, like a fresh Polaroid, blurry as I see it most times. I wonder, am I to ever be normal and able to complete my life script without changing the lines as written for me to be happy and ultimately find success?

Patience, I hear often.

I hear the word *patience* whispered in the wind as I wander from place to place. Patience is a place I struggle living near since we live in a gratitude now or even better, yesterday type of world. A world where you can post or share your immediate life, get reception from the masses in the blink of an eye, and receive instant gratification. Patience, while I wonder, will I ever give love wholly and properly in the rarest of forms?

Am I able to give love intimately to someone else who is willing to reciprocate the actions not by tone alone but by moving in unison alongside my being for a journey into forever? This is yet to be seen, but my faith says God makes no mistakes.

Even though mines have sent me on a painful detour, I have faith God will provide better and hope that my issues are simply a blueprint for the world to see that when you place your faith in his hands and you act accordingly, with lots of work, you can overcome your own self-sabotage and be the example of a love you disregarded or never in life had.

I plan on going deep into my bag within this reading (my journal) to discuss my own personal actions and how I came to the place I now sit.

Deep in regret, it is here I have the opportunity to speak on things randomly without pointing a finger. There is no structure, I am rambling, I write as the emotions present themselves, so excuse my constant shifts in subject matter or time frames. This is a reflection of hurt; the information is a lifelong journey that's finally been given permission to exit the womb, symbolic of birth as I write.

I apologize to no one for my random form of discussion. To all I have hurt, I am truly sorry for my actions. Note, I suffer intensely today for my faults in the past. I do apologize, sincerely!

Wholeheartedly I want to own my actions in a way I have never been able to—brash, out loud, and in the open. Silence was considered a safe space for me. I used silence to run and hide as that little boy did when he had to confront life's variables. Silence became my friend when there weren't any. It was the place where you just be. In silence, I found that my thoughts and old actions were able to sit at the table of life and have a candid and unscripted conversation about each other and find resolution to the many problems about my life.

Since it was a direct reflection of what I thought safe was, I now have been forced once again to sit, silently. Now it is truly unwanted. Silence has become the driving force behind my shifts in emotions compounded with the guilt I carry as I think constantly back on my life obstacles. It is this silence that allows for my current self-reflection that usually is so intense I have to open completely up and accept the good, the bad, and the ugly of myself.

If you have not guessed it yet, the majority of this reading will be about my adventures with the word *love*. It's the lead topic of conversation, not to explain old issues and shift blame or excuse my actions, I just want to express what I believe is the root of my own inabilities as a man to properly use it for its beauty. The reasons why I have made poor decisions with it and how I understand the impact it had on so many lives. Most important is realizing why I decided to act and what I learned from the positive and, more important, the negative moments from my battles.

Love is harsh and has its hurdles; it's warm and necessary. Love is needed by all and confusing; it's used to hurt and uplift and can be done all in the same moments. Love is what we all need, had, have, and pursue just as much as any other tangible items, for it's love that one can sustain on like air and water without material if it is harnessed with the right person for the right reason in the right moments. I guess that's why they say love conquers all.

Love by definition in *Webster* (noun)—it is an intense feeling of deep affection. To have a great interest and pleasure in something. A person or thing that one loves.

Love by definition in *Webster* (verb)—feeling deep affection for (someone). To like or enjoy very much.

Love, a word so often thrown around in social circles loosely. Personally, I wondered how it would take shape to eventually impact and mold me as a man.

How could this one word complete me as a person? Being in it was something I wrestled with because its meanings in my eyes were faint as whispers heard from a distance.

Oftentimes, I overlooked several important yet missing parts of love because it was an inevitable expectation due circumstances; love was just supposed to be relevant. No time to ponder on the reasoning, just be prepared. Since I felt a natural lack of it growing up, this led to my manipulation of it and future misuse. Faking it most times as an adult due my knowledgeable ignorance. I hardly ever understood if it is or was real when I possessed it, often like a thief, since I probably acquired it outside my vows or halfheartedly assumed that it was there in a flashy unique form just hanging around in the shadows lurking over my shoulders.

I was reckless with it due my inexperience, and usually I passed it along without regard of the intense actions it would have on the mind, body, and soul of not only myself but, more important, the person receiving it on the other end.

How could I?

I mean there's no manual that comes alongside its acquisition or space on your birth certificate which states your love levels. No warning label you can canvass like the food from the grocery store.

Love is unquantifiable and optimally, I believed, learned by trial and error as we all have our chase of its glory throughout life.

I normally disregarded others' feelings because I had mixed emotions; most times I placed myself in a position where at a minimum, I cared. The bigger issue was I ensured both parties cared; and that has always been the bridge that created future damage as the moments were surreal, but the aftermath was that equal to some of the world's most horrific storms without any help from the outside for the clean-up.

I would compartmentalize and move forward to the next place, with the same damage, prepared to set new fires that only added to the existent flames of pain. Plus, I had no control over their mind and emotional IQ in regard to the giving and receiving of love (we are all grown was my thinking).

Please, before you read on, inhale, exhale, and just take a moment.

Grab a sheet of paper, open your notepad on your phone, or simply sit and answer me this. What does the word *love* actually mean individually to you? Not what the definition is, I provided it for us on purpose in its generic form so we can all have basic understanding of the concept of the word. There is more to the word *love* once you include your life's journey, history, and personal experiences. When you wrestle with the emotional roller coaster it has taken you on and you take the time to reflect on how it has had an impact on your life, the shift from the generic definition takes shape.

Due this fact, I want you to dig deep inside your history and think about what it means to you and only you when you reflect on your past. Think about being in it, growing up with or without it, what your picture of it looks like, and maybe how you gave and give it out or received and accepted it in all its unique forms and fashions. Now I ask you again, what does the word *love* really mean to you?

If you are as honest as I am, well, this will be an interesting read as we journey into my data banks and unpack some boxes I have held in my head Rolodex for too long. I thank you in advance for allowing my journey to be shared in a form that most Black men do not usually share. I believe that this is my first step in not only finding some closure with my skeletons but also finding the forgiveness of self that I need to continue on this journey into a life of being well-respected not only as a man but as a humble man of my faith.

We all have sin attached to our names. To have a dialogue about my own sin is the first in a number of steps in becoming a better person, a better friend, and future partner. Who knows, my future wife may read this, and she will understand the man. She just may understand that the man she is with actually has a gentle heart, is very much able to love, and only needed a like-minded soul to be beside him day in and out. That he didn't ask to walk these lines drunk in love his entire life. He really wanted to find a love that was rightfully for him in a sober and love-free-mind state.

A love that was equal to his in all aspects and that he already pursued several and failed; to fall in it, exclusively with her and her alone at the right time. He was now completely rid of the guilt he carried, the blame and the games to find himself at peace, and in a place that his scars would not be excuses for an escape but the blueprint for a love so unimaginable that each day would feel like a dream.

A love that she will thank God alone for the damage done him as the ability to properly be was only available do to his many prior issues, failures, and faults. He was done with the games of children and finally ready and actually able to be a man. He learned from a love that was built one mistake after another by his own choices.

He was placed in her life at a time where a love at its worst in life was now by the hands of God, rebuilt in faith, and could properly perform at its best with her as a unit because we both long to be loved. We both are alone and scared to love, yet we both ultimately are tired of that unwashed space in the center our spines we use tools and foreign objects to reach. We hope to simply find one worthy of trusting with our secrets and stories of old pain. We only want to walk in peace and tranquility knowing we are secure with ourselves and will wash each other's backs of the dirt we both can't reach.

Origins and History of Love Retrieved from the Etymology Dictionary

> love (n.) Old English *lufu* "feeling of love; romantic sexual attraction; affection; friendliness; the love of God; Love as an abstraction or personification," from Proto-Germanic **lubo* (source also of Old High German *liubi* "joy," German *liebe* "love;" Old Norse, Old Frisian, Dutch *lof*, German *lob* "praise;" Old Saxon *liof*, Old Frisian *liaf*, Dutch *lief*, Old High German *liob*, German *lieb*, Gothic *liufs* "dear, beloved"). The Germanic words are from PIE root *leubh*—"to care, desire, love."

My online research shows that the word *love* is stated 310 times in the King James Version of the Bible, and this number fluctuates dependent upon which version you frequent or follow, but the ultimate point is that it is so relevant in spiritual teachings that it could only mean it be a significant part in our daily lives as well.

From the beginning, we are taught God himself is the ultimate form of love. He encompasses all the word is to mean, for God is love. That should be all, single, no more, no less. We in human form feel the need to reassess things to fit our modern-day conclusions and lifestyles. Terms are changed to fit earthly needs, and exceptions to standards take shape. The word is shifted to meet personal needs as I often manipulated and mixed it in with my own sins.

You can find several original versions and meanings of the word in study such as eros, storge, philia, and agape.

Eros is that love you have in a romantic or sensual form. It is the one most often longed for and yet the one we most often take full advantage of. Eros was originally put into play for those who were married as a way to continue to experience their unity as a couple, physically in tune for a higher purpose as one connected unit. This form of love has since been taken and used out of the norm, for it is a known sin to experience an eros-type love without properly being one under God with your mate.

Storge is the love we are born with, for we seek it from birth in our *familia* or families; naturally all having a sense of it due the birthright. A genuine love because we are personally interconnected by genetics which is blood tied to us from the tree of life we share with others in our life cycle. Parents have children, and a bond is formed. Those children have children, and an extension to that bond is created. The cycle continues, and through the cycle, it is learned behavior that this is family and/or blood, and we are one to survive in the world as a unit. Storge is a love that makes you commit to things out of an obligation. You have this love which causes you to act due responsibility it feels or simply just because.

Storge is that tough love because it is not tied to a feeling but a code. We are a unit; we are family, and so I love you. I have issues at times with storge love because I am very much an emotional male, and I tend to tie my feelings to actions. It has always been hard for me to just simply love one more than another just because of titles and codes. I have had people do more for me throughout my lifetime than any one in my immediate extended family, yet this is just me because in the same breath, I can say I know a lot of individuals who have and had family they would give it all for because they played a real part in their lives at some time.

We all are unique and walk separate paths on purpose, and mine, well, it didn't afford me much storge love from top to bottom, sometimes due geographics, others because of resources; no one was to blame, and so other forms took place.

Philia is the love that God requires man to have amongst each other while we play our parts here on earth. We are all required to ensure we display this type of love daily while we perform our duties as servants on earth, and yet this is a love seldom seen utilized in the fashion God expected. From the daily hellos to the assist of one in need, it is far-reaching and ever so impactful to the recipient we forget how it gives the owner fuel for a better tomorrow.

It is a genuine ability to look at one not from your bloodline as a brother or sister in life. An extension of humanity, giving a hand when and if it is ever necessary as you would do to your own.

Philia is seen in many relationships and is often one that eventually grows into an eros as relationships grow in their unique directions. It often crosses lines in a sinful manner, but yet it is the basis and ground floor to a healthy relationship, for without philia, there cannot in my eyes be a healthy eros after marriage as those loves intersect each other in a healthy way.

To find peace knowing that you have love for another person because they simply are and not because you have a need is a unique gift.

Last but not least is agape love. Agape love is the one I most have had my difficulties with not fully grasping the importance of its use. This is the highest of the four forms as this is the love that God has for us as his children. It is unconditional as he understands the sin we bear and the fault we have. He does not judge, for his love is everlasting and never changing as it was written.

Agape love is not weak or soft; it does not tie into your emotional IQ or have a sexual or intimate tone. Agape love defies all that we could ever assume love would be as it is the pinnacle of something we would never be able to achieve due to earthly flaws. It is nothing and everything wrapped in one as a base; it just is! It is all of who God is.

God loves because God is love; that is His nature and the way He has always presented Himself to us. God is love! It's a place we strive to be, yet we continually fail and fall short as we will never have the ability to reach such great potential. His sacrifice of self was and is still to this day the epitome of what love could ever be no matter what form you choose to use.

He loves all the saints and the sinners as we find it hard to simply love thy neighbor. The prophets and the peasants, believe it or not, He loves us all the same, not because we deserve it but because it is His nature to love.

God must always be Him, so He must be true to Himself, or in other words, God always keeps it 100 as He is what love is.

The four terms above were retrieved from other sources. I added my own twist inclusive with their writings and changed some of the format to fit my style and make it my own.

I am sorry in advance if the owners may assume I have detoured from their originals or added my own words to deviate from what they believe. I placed it here for others looking for understanding about love and its different meanings aside of myself. This gives us the ability to distinguish the individual emotions we exude and assist with linking into a love with God. Like myself, you may not understand love and might get overwhelmed like I did.

It may be hard to believe it exists. I, too, struggle with things, especially information I can't properly comprehend. I believe the art of faith comes into play. I'm not a minister or evangelist, but I do believe in its accuracy and hope it has an impact and helps us both better understand the love of God.

Do you ever wonder why life seems so difficult to live? You awake looking off into the forefront of existence with hope you have the ability to tackle all that is in your day, and this happens even before you set one foot onto the ground.

The angst is upon you, and the tone for the next twenty-four hours is preset. You inhale slow and exhale with ease while forcing yourself to maneuver from your bed.

The irony is that most often times we have so much pinned inside from recent nights and prior days, weeks before, and months that past.

Weight carried inside from years of pain seem like several lifetimes. Pressure resides in small spaces which are strategically stored inside your head, card-catalogued in perfect order.

Each day you arise finding strength to face your unknown. Echoes ring aloud. You dread the day ahead and fear having to glance into what tomorrow is to add to the list of issues that currently hold residence in your mind.

Get right is the current thought, while you look at your reflection in the mirror, eventually moving forward in a zombie-like fashion with a smile, the same smile that gained compliment from the souls you would eventually tie into.

Repetition of work, school, bills, clubbing, streets, friends, relationship issues, politics, kids, family, social media distractions to include the acceptance we all chase, the influence from the outside, and boxes we hide. The truth is, you are battered, bruised, confused, and worn. The wrongs and secrets are draining; it's a mission to awaken with a smile and move steadfast into the blessing which is your future, aka the next day.

I found myself walking dead, drained and broken, so engulfed with a woman that I allowed my mind to lose itself as we once were the picture of excellence—at least that is what I would often tell myself.

It was a joy to remove myself from the covers and gallop into whatever life had to throw at me each morning because I thought my forever was there. I assumed I found the one thing we all long for. I fought my storms for what I believed was *love*!

My sad reality is that it was never to be. It was not prewritten in my plan, so no matter how hard I fought to make it mine, unfortunately, it was already a dead-end situation. Imagine walking without instruction to a nowhere ahead, with hopes you could rewrite the script. The Band-Aids I placed on my life all eventually were removed. I now sit in disgust at myself because I eventually gave up on me, and most importantly, I still carried hate and blame, as I gave up on God.

I am not the most knowledgeable speaker on the subject of spirituality and the ways of God. I do not claim to be a scholar as it pertains to the Bible and what the word speaks as to be truth for our basic ways of life. My ignorance, I own, and I live in confusion as I've always allowed man to provide insight to the word. I don't have the ability to quote scripture and use my tone to throw verses sporadically at you like darts to make you believe. I am you as you read, *a sinner*. I am a sinner who has sinned throughout life, and I own my faults.

The difference is that while I sit in solitude, I understand that if you truly need to find peace in yourself, the one common denominator will always have to be a steady relationship humbly with God.

I grew up in the church as it was a second home; my family tree was the church. Everyone sanctified and very active in all aspects of servitude from pastors, trustees, choir directors, mothers, board members, deacons, evangelistic servants, traveling speakers, choir members, musicians, writers of the word, and so much more.

I gradually understood differences with spirituality and what my religious beliefs were and who I was to the church growing up.

I can relate to praise and prayer as scripted; and what part it is to play in our daily lives but the one thing I didn't have until now is a daily back and forth on a personal level with God. I didn't until now have a daily interaction with Him just as I would anyone else in this world. I actually placed Him in a box that said break only when needed.

I fight daily with God in a fashion that is tiring as life seems to be a fraction of what it once was. Often, I confuse my spiritual relationship with a need to be dressed in a suit and tie or holding the scripture to properly present myself. I confused it with the many nights the blue lights flashed behind me and I was in an immediate need or I got some bad news and looked for a way out. I confuse it now as I hurt and have an emotional pain I continue to carry like no other, with what seems like no ear in sight so my cries for peace feel unheard and for not.

Honestly, I had so many dark secrets and lies that I amassed inside my head that I think I was simply too embarrassed to talk with him due my behavior—I mean, you wouldn't tell your parents your darkest moments in life, so how on earth could you tell not only someone you have never met before but the supreme being Himself your dirt and lies.

I forgot that God is all-seeing and knowing. I forgot that before my mistakes were made, He knew my path and that the mistake was going to be made; the test was, would I come to Him for guidance to resolve my issues?

Would I ask Him for support and, more importantly, forgiveness? Would I be able to bear down in my time of need and speak with Him as freely as I spoke to the people alongside my life daily?

God as we know is extremely jealous and wants us to seek Him for support and not the ones we so often confide in daily who usually carry their own crosses unexposed in life. I believe He wants us to call and not only when in need but daily and often.

Like I said, I'm not a spiritual guru or Bible thumper, but I do seriously believe. Even in my darkest of moments while I sit alone every day confused wondering what my life is for, I do believe. I believe I am loved and lack direction; I am lost and being subjected to trials that will ensure I have peace moving forward. I understand that even if it isn't worth much in the public's eye, my life story in whole is a survival kit. The birth and life of a damaged man, his numerous escapes with death and the adversities in tow. I have been able to overcome, even though I feel like I am less than a man and lost in society; I feel God grants me favor.

I believe to this day from my birth; God saw and still sees so much more in me and expects the same from me because I am still here and able to sit and present these emotions to the online world, and that in itself, as sad as I am, is my blessing.

So I challenge you as I have been challenged to take the time each day as you arise to find a minute to give to the Creator. Before you reach for that phone looking to find yourself some temporary satisfaction or before you head to the bathroom to sit and plot on the day's mission, before you turn the TV on, get started with family, friends, and get consumed with the noise of the world as hard as it may be; give thanks and have a conversation.

You are not alone because daily, it's a fight to be consistent.

Breathe. Now take a moment and think about how far you have come and how far you might go if you and I only have the courage to give God His praise regardless of the current state of affairs, regardless our current situation, and regardless our life's obstacles.

Think about it. We just might find the same things that are holding us back are the same things He placed in our way in hopes that we would simply remember who He was and love Him as much as He loves us. I have been on the opposite end of a one-way love, a love where you feel you are giving and giving and never receiving.

If God sent Jesus to earth in human form so that He may understand in heaven what we feel as emotions, then I believe He does know the pain I sit in; He knows my heart and how I currently feel. He also knows where I lack and that I show little faith in my spiritual body. He knows that I have withheld love and that I lack love toward Him after all He has done for me.

Though this may seem small in text, I hope your eyes translate the words into songs that dance in your thoughts after you have read and they then become latched to your memory. He only wants to be loved. Think about it, *who doesn't?*

I am learning this the hard way, and as much as it hurts, I believe it is necessary for me to heal and move forward.

A simple unscripted prayer, regardless of sin, simply believe.

Thank You, Jesus, for all you have done and the lengths you have went to provide. Thank You for covering my past transgressions and sins so that I may have a clean slate in your eyes. Please help me heal from the past so that I may have a clear understanding of the future, and know even though I am not perfect, I will strive for perfection in hopes to one day be by your side. Amen.

Learn Religions says that

> In the Bible we learn that Jesus Christ demonstrated this kind of divine love to his Father and to all humanity in the way he lived and died: "For God so loved the world, that he gave his only Son, that whoever believes in him should not perish but have eternal life." (John 3:16)

> Following his resurrection, Jesus asked the apostle Peter if he loved him (agape). Peter replied three times that he did, but the word he

used was phileo or brotherly love (John 21:15–19). Peter had not yet received the Holy Spirit at Pentecost; he was incapable of agape love. But after Pentecost, Peter was so full of God's love that he spoke from his heart and 3,000 people were converted

Love is one of the most powerful emotions humans can experience. For Christian believers, love is the truest test of genuine faith. Through the Bible, we discover how to experience love in its many forms and to share it with others as God intended. (Jack Zavada, "4 Types of Love in the Bible," learnreligions.com, 2021)

What inside of us is love ultimately connected to, I truly believe it is more than just the heart. What outside of us forces our beings to detach from ourselves to so often fight so hard for it or flee so fast and easily from it?

Why did I, or do I need it to survive in this world, a world where we find it easier to not simply love thy neighbor as God requires of us? I notice that our society has created a norm where we as a collective group fail over and over.

Why are we so selective of who is and who is not to be loved, having the nerve to define and reason with our internal selves as to question what God actually meant when He stated in the simplest of forms that we should all love our neighbors as we would expect them to love us in return. It's reciprocity 101 in a form that could change the current state of affairs in a world where learned behavior makes it easier to hate another's being, vice enjoying each as if we are one.

Why do I feel so in tune with my piece of the world when I have it, and if it is so important to us as an intricate part of our humanity and makeup, how and why should I give it up aside of God's will? Again, I am far from an evangelist or experienced theologist, but his request I can understand. Agape, eros, philia, and storge are all words I can comprehend the meanings of. They all in some way, shape, or form resonate specifically with several of my own life instances.

Love "Better Learned Forty-eight Years Later, Vice Never"

I wonder why the latter wasn't the basis of my first understandings some forty-plus years ago about love so that it could become learned behavior, vice a learned after the fact of failure emotional fix.

In school, I would have rather had a full-on class about any and everything involving love. All of its ins and outs. Story after story about its daily part of our emotional lives and culture. As I see it, I wasted years of my life learning the history of a nation that doesn't acknowledge my existence. I learned much about things which are today being hidden due their ugliness and impact on truth as our world is reshaped. I spent countless hours shaping my fragile mind in the search of answers to the letters A+B and how they equal C. They have never made me any more successful in life and have never ever once been used constructively as a survival skill during my adulthood, let alone in a way to accumulate resources for personal gain; but love, yeah, this love thing has been in each and every corner of my life daily.

No rocks thrown or blame passed to anyone or anything. I blame me. My lack of an ongoing and unforced spiritual foundation will be my blame I place. It is all on me!

The information just as I sought it out now was present then, I am sure. I simply chose to not look for it. So easily and often in life without a fight to accomplish a win or to achieve some momentary goal which had nothing to do with my now, I would play my part in a wrestling match of love amongst another.

The root of the situation was that in some way, shape, or form where love was an added ingredient in the equation, my lack or over-abundance of its use was pivotal in several outcomes which have led me to a place where numb becomes an aftereffect due the intrinsic and extrinsic abuse of it.

While restless and tossing in bed trying to find my way to sleep, I lay in silence as I often do after a long boring day of wrestling back and forth with my past and current insecurities. It was during this isolated session that I felt an overwhelming need to reach for my cellphone which I use when an idea is apparent. I opened it, one eye shut with a dim light, and I felt compelled to type this.

In reference to love, "You will never fully become who you are to be in it if you continue to dwell on the person you previously were in it."

As I arise, I ponder on what this meant. What was being said to my subconscious? Who placed it here or there and why at that immediate moment? What was I to do? Why was a statement so simple yet prolific in tone entrusted to my penmanship, the very same person who has been struggling with love? It was what I like to call a "God moment." Those moments in time when you are at your worst, and after reaching and clawing for resolution at the most awkward of times, you hear something, you see something, your thoughts are given, you accomplish something without any effort, and you're blessed with resource or something as simple as a word placed on your mind and heart for it to be understood.

God moments, yes, even the worst of us have them. We most times are so wrapped up in life that we choose to not see them or acknowledge them until we are alone or at our last.

As for the statement, in my reply, I thought:

To me, this means that we all have adversity and struggles we attach our thoughts to in order to process and then try to proceed in life. The statement "learning from your mistakes" comes to mind.

Failure is an obstacle each and every one of us has had to battle at a given point throughout our existence. To be fully engulfed in what you are to accomplish in life in any given realm, you must find unique ways to block out the noise and fight for what is yours in the world. If that means hard attempts at letting your prior battles move on after you have taken the time to consult with yourself about issues and mishaps, then you must.

The main point is to learn from prior actions to help create a better self for future use. It is in these moments you reflect and retrain, so moving forward you are not left wondering what happened and/or what went wrong in the case things are not as you plan.

I often failed resting in those pits, and that consumed my being. Those dark moments and memories helped me to create my plans that would eventually act as plots to be used, if necessary.

Plots that I could use to simply move laterally into another position without an emotional shutdown or overbearing heartache. These are the moments that leave the gaps I will speak about later on.

Remember, if you continue to find fault in your past life, you will never be able to find fruit in your future life. You will always look at any and everything that transpires as a plot against you because you live your life one foot in and one foot out. This is destructive behavior and allows you not only to plan for the worst, but your actions will most definitely begin to reflect your intricate plot as time will reveal all.

To be in love is learning that your prior issues do not always play an immediate role in your current issues; your actions do. If you are walking the path the same way as you did before, this may be the fact that you never adjusted who you were from what you learned.

If you sit in it long enough, you will see that looking back and learning does not mean looking back and reliving, as I often assumed was the way forward.

I would live my life as if I had a small sample size of actions to reach back and look at before any major decision was to be made, wondering if the escapes from circumstances would change if I made small tweaks and shifts to my parts played from my history.

The only problem is, in love, there aren't any two situations which are exactly alike because we are dealing with subjects that are not the same. No matter how much you assume the picture is painted perfect, you must remember: a replicate will never equal an original, for one of one means just that—it is one.

Love, love, love. Love is a word I loathe most in life, right next to a few other choice nouns and verbs which consistently shed the brightest light on my insecurities and fears. I have grown to believe the word is significantly hollow and numbing on purpose as the world around me uses it shamelessly and at other times strategically and with purpose and direction because one is seasoned in the subject unlike myself.

I often would view love through the eyes of others in conversations and discussions where I had opportunities to see just as the other person needed to for their personal flights in life. I would eventually be forced to sit in it suffering in silence from what I believed was a constant lack of it especially in my younger years as I grew up leading to adolescence and the terrible circumstances all inner-city youth face via lack of resources, lack of material wealth, instabilities in the household, systematic racism, and the ongoing outside judgment we often face from our innocent but knowing peers.

See, for a lifetime, love never seemed readily accessible to me or even at arm's length much of what I can recall. I never really seemed to have full grasp or complete access to it in its purest of forms, yet I had taken the time to canvass several books on the subject growing up. Books about what it was supposed to be. The songs of the good, bad, and ugly along with what to expect from it.

I mimicked popular artist from numerous genres of music about what it sounded like and what I should say to access its overflow, just in case I got lucky enough to hit the right notes or find some sort of popularity where it was thrown at me freely in an artificial manner because of my never-met-up-to social status.

I scanned magazines and watched a multitude of fairy tales on screen, television shows, and the such, falling in like with story lines, plots, and twist. Watching and reading characters play their roles to replicate real scenes in what love was to be. From behind the writer's lines, these theatrics led me to purposely believe in all the happiness associated with it, especially the fake adversity and pain you endure to fight for it. I was always left to ignorantly believe my own analogy, that time held the key to its ever-revolving doors, and if you held on and persevered the race, ultimately life had this red tape, a finish line which was awaiting you to crash your heart across in the end because love never fails and always ends with happiness, hugs, kisses, and joy! Right?

I was introduced to what I thought was a form of it in the watching of pornography behind my parents' backs at a very young age. A classmate a couple grades ahead of me would often pop up with some material we would watch and study for our own future acts with females.

His father had a trunk full of VHS tapes in a locker, and I can recall everyone encouraging me to watch at my home; since my room was in the basement, we figured we had a safe space. It was my first dose of selective coolish, I call it. I wasn't popular or the cool guy amongst those I considered to be my comrades or close buds; I was being used because I had a resource, and back then, who would've known this would be my first introduction to what users do? My room was in the basement of our Midwest home, and it was the entire basement minus the laundry room. All the guys would come by because it was private, and we could be us without judgment, freedom to be kids and mischievous.

I would act as if I was the ring leader in control of the week's gift to our underdeveloped brain cells and the lead instructor in a Sex 101 course for our semester term. Floor model big back television was warmed up, RCA VHS cables intact, power on, and we got action. I think back and now see the beginnings to future struggles of many men.

We would space ourselves out away from each other as if to keep some man code intact, sit, and watch in amazement at how they were so free and just in the act of what I thought was love and how it was physically made. I would handle the controls of the volume so my sickly mother couldn't overhear the moans and groans, turning it up and down on purpose to bother the viewers in the room, but actually I believe I did it because I was often excited about the action, and this was a good deflection.

As a preteen and coming off an ugly ordeal at an earlier age which plays vague in my mind, I openly welcomed the videos because they represented what I knew love to emulate and not what

I happened to be subject to. This is what love was supposed to look like even if it was not real; it surely looked and definitely sounded like it felt good to those involved. I was all in and hooked not just because of what I was watching but because it looked interesting to me. I would make sure to keep my composure until they left, which was typically shortly after the tapes got good cause we all couldn't be sitting around with our hormones on, ten so usually after a few minutes, someone would excuse themselves, and the rest would follow, and I would always ensure I would keep the tape until the next link-up and swap-out session.

What have I now gotten myself into? This is the answer to the issues I believe I have. I would study the tapes alone after all would leave as if I was next on the set. I had to get my moves perfected for the part I was about to play in life. The bulge in my pants as I watched reassured me that I was turned on.

I was looking at what I assumed love was, and it was what I wanted because it, like a switch, turned me on, and I believed that I was right to feel how I did as I looked at the females in the videos.

At these delicate brain-forming moments of my life, I didn't have scriptures in my head, though I was a church kid for sure. I didn't see this as the sin it is; I saw my short past and what had happened in my life. I saw the pain and agony of a child who had a secret, fearful of telling anyone else. I consumed myself with the thought of what I believed love was.

It showed me something my internal spirit needed. It gave me hope to be normal. The natural setback was I wasn't having sex at that age; this all transpired and created an intense curiosity that was savage. First comes the touch and the feel. Then masturbation begins, and the devil finds his way slowly into your mindset and way of thinking. You don't know it yet, but the evil is now forming in your being as a tool to try and hinder your life. The sins are now working internally and are parallel and alongside the original tool, and you begin a masturbation ritual. From the time it will happen to the people you're with in your head and places you are at as it goes down.

You get consumed with the act and the feeling it gives off as it is nothing like the memories you fight with from your childhood. You end up envisioning yourself and others from stars and artist, entertainers, classmates, even the prettiest women from the neighborhood were all in your self-played out fantasies.

I knew the tapes and my experiments were not real. It was like daydreaming to me, simply all in my head. I would oftentimes look in amazement at those tapes though, watching and studying the moves because it was better than acting; they were also teaching me firsthand what I should do when I got me some love.

Or so I thought.

I'm glad I came into myself, and life changed my mindset for the moment because I think these are the moments where boys are so vulnerable and have the potential of becoming physical predators and sexual deviants when these emotions are left unchecked or therapy is unprovided. I happened to have a strong will and now believe it was God himself who placed me on a time-out from myself so that an inner-city kid could avoid the destruction that typically follows along with the activity I was exposed to.

I was once again saved, and I truly believe that God placed other things in my life to remove the stench of lust from my being. I became an avid chess player and made the papers a couple times and got into sports and accomplished a lot as baseball became an everyday part of my life from a preteen until my departure for service.

The only problem with exposure is it is there, and it happened. I believe it was not gone but now simply inside me. That stench was now a part of my makeup, and though controlled, wanting my own version of intimacy was there and waiting. I wanted to be with someone; I wanted to share in a like love experience what love was in my eyes.

Even in growth, as I finally assumed I knew what it felt like, the face it had, its smell and sound, how it cared and considered me an equal, see that one, right there, that love, see that love is the one that hurts and isn't anything like the above. I will say with a wrinkled brow that the pain as I sit currently in, with all due respect for the word, I now know who you are, love, or at least I can say I know what my version of you has been, currently is, and hopefully will not continue to be.

The HuffPost states:

> Love is painful, because it creates the way for joy, for bliss and for compassion. Love is painful, because it transforms you. Love is growth. **Love itself does not hurt. It is growth that hurts, the ego that stings.**
>
> Each transformation is painful because the old situation is being left behind for the new. For example, when a relationship ends, we feel hurt, our hopes and dreams have crashed and we feel lost and lonely, wondering what comes next. Fear arises because the unknown is in front of us, and the mind usually assumes the negative, saying things like, "I'll never meet anyone else," "I'm too old/overweight/unattractive" or "I don't have time for a new relationship." The temptation is to shut down, open that bag of potato chips, pour that glass of wine, turn on the TV and give up on love.

Crazy as it sounds, this is the exact way I feel; it was as if they were peeking into the windows of my mind and pulling a screenshot of my every thought out prior to writing their analogy into print.

But what about God? What do we do when the love we are not looking for is placed in your purview. What happens when it's more of a spiritual love that is being ultimately manifested, something you know nothing about because your prior way of life was filled with so many miscues and fallacies of its essence? How do we shift when we want earthly love because it is what we have grown to feel completes us and God has an alternate plan?

He faces you one on one and says, "If you want to live an honest life, you must first understand my love and all it is." "You have to show me you are capable of change and want to be involved in what

I planned as your life script." "Love, as I require, will challenge who you have become, so for you to journey on, you must submit and rebuild before you are forced to face yourself, and I make the change for you,"

That change, by the time you query, is already in work and apparent. The bigger issue as the flesh fights to conform is humans hate when they feel they are okay where they currently are, and change, well, it truly isn't necessary unless it involves a person, place, or thing which helps us to feel a step ahead of our yesterday and closer to a better tomorrow.

How do we deal with the unknown, those things we cannot see or feel outside of our own reality? What about the movement away from what we as people think is love, those random breakups when things were perfect in your eyes? While on my voyage, I stopped and found a safe space in Huntsville with my parents on a mission to heal. It was not what I chose, but what was placed in the cards as I chased healing and there, I faced some extreme and intense emotional baggage. I was thrust back into a painful past and childhood I hated to relive in conversation. I unleashed years of held-back pain and tales from the history they only knew pieces, if that about.

They often listened in awe and apologized about what was done or not on their behalf, and in the end, we all were torn and battered and, in my heart, I believe a little worse off than if I had said nothing at all. As I went back and forth daily with my parents about life, lack, love, and where I believe things went array, it felt like I was blaming them vice explaining to them. Some days were good, but most were bad as I realized after being gone for thirty years, we didn't even know each other as most families do. We were a shell of the family we were at one point. Nothing like that storge love spoke on earlier as it felt we were blood-tied and nothing more. I grew extremely frustrated as this couldn't be what life was meant to be. I left for military as directed due my past transgressions and failed street activity in search of a way to support the child I fathered, but not in hopes to lose my family.

One night I decided to attend a church service hoping to share in a moment I knew would be a safe space for them, comfort zone, and a renewed moment for myself. Here I met Pastor Clayborn Lea. He was visiting from California, and to me it was an opportunity to be with my mother like the days of old, hoping it would insight something in her and me to create some unique tie we could turn into a spark to a new us.

The pastor gave an amazing sermon, and we sang and rejoiced, and it was better than I could imagine actually. The joy on her face was priceless, and I felt enamored to be in her presence as she fought her pain to attend service and support in person. I took notes and listened to each word, and ending, the pastor gave us a brief story about his personal battle with cancer. He told us how he was proactive with his health and considered a healthy man, and suddenly he was forced to battle for his life. He turned his fears into fight and eventually overcame his obstacles, but it cost him.

This resonated with my soul, and I sat wondering if the pastor was broken and went through a process to survive. I am doomed. I met him after and took photos and purchased his book, which I will say is very much enlightening, but at the time, my mindset was if the man who pastors and passes on firsthand God's word is battling for his life, I know I am in trouble. This was another dark moment moving forward for me as I felt like I would be the last on a list of people God would care to deal with.

This would be a turning point for me, and it wasn't just the meeting and his story of grace and survival; it wasn't the opportunity to be with my parents as the days of old or the realization and affirmation that my life isn't any less than his, though we took different routes to end up in the same church to praise God.

It was because it showed me that life is unique, and the interactions and stories we gather from the passersby have substance which can tie life together for us as we move through each day. I didn't know him, and if I had not made the attempt to get closer to my broken family, I would have not had opportunity to get my hands on a book that would help move me on in my life journey.

Giant Lessons from David is a book he penned and was selling after service, and my purchase at the time was support of another African American businessman. Little did I know it would eventually become a piece of literature that would help clarify some of my darkest questions and struggles with God at a time where I figured death would be more satisfying vice fighting to live for the next day as I expected it to be as painful as the last.

Pastor Lea made justification to this fact that there are crutches we all create in life to help us get from point A to point B and use of these so-called crutches hinders our personal, professional, and spiritual growth, after all the glitz and glamour settles in. We become reliant on things and forget that we are to love God and show him favor for all that he has done for us in the blessings we receive.

I broke down into tears after reading because my life was blown up exactly in the order of his examples. First, I was not selected for advancement in a job I knew for a fact I was properly prepared to take; I was ranked number one. And as the number one candidate coming off a very successful tour of duty more than once, I was not selected. While others with blemishes and flaws in their records were not only promoted but celebrated, I felt I was sent off to expire.

After retiring, I leaned on a different type of love; it was that of relationship and friends. The love crutches were ultimately and out of the blue shifted and removed, so then were the so-called friends which all originally were corelated with my successful military career.

In the matter of a few years, I not only lost opportunity at continuing my beloved career, I lost the love of my personal life, loves I carried throughout my days, and the friends associated with that same life.

I finished the chapter hurt and with tears in my eyes because I couldn't understand. Why place me in a numb emotional state confused as to how life would be? Left once again turned upside down. My only reasoning was my lack of a relationship with God throughout it all, as I was simply going through the motions day in and day out.

Reverend Lea's book on David is an amazing tale of how he was selected for a specific reason eventually finding his purpose, and that purpose was to become a great servant, directly to and for God's ultimate script, but the life he endured had several unforeseen twists and turns. He went from the bottom to the top, from shepherd to savior.

No money to more money, I guess. All for his valiant efforts, but in doing so, he was removed from all he knew and had to adjust to his newfound successes, for he was on a path of sin that was his to own.

His fight eventually led him to accomplish things that were way larger than he could ever imagine and done alone. He found his place with God. He was a real believer and ensured he kept a consistent and open dialogue with God at all times. Out of all the reading, the one thing I focused on was his life of sin and yet praise for God.

He was a sinner, and he knew God knew his plight, yet he still found time to sing God his praise often and out loud with zero shame. I do not know if this bought him favor or was his nature, but God saw fit; he was able to sustain and live a good life. He allowed him to go from a man of little to no means to eventually become a king and rule. This is where I find hope in that God knows my heart.

I pray he finds a moment to show me favor as he did David and allows for me to live a better life understanding I am not my past but that I can be a better person because of it.

I sit looking at my life and how it is under an assault and wonder what is it that I may have done to be placed in this position. Am I that bad of a person that my removal is necessary because I have sinned and made love a crutch in all aspects of my life as an imposter? Hopefully, we all can one day read this and say God had a plan that was bigger than my immediate need to be who I was, and I was able to fight my past and prevail in my future, but to be detached from all you know creates the delusion that I am in a never-ending time-out because of the faults I placed on myself and others which currently prolong my destiny.

This is a memoir of words and script that, Lord willing, I pray I can reflect on in old age and say to myself, look at God, look at how God took a man that was internally set aflame, picked him up as He promised, and dusted him off to represent him in a better fashion to his world. Look at how God stood by His word and accepted this man consumed with sin, yet because of his love, He spared him from darkness to be an example in this life. Look at how God took His child and placed him ten toes down, not up, as he continues to walk in life freshly equipped with a new set of tools to become not only a servant but a better man as he travels around each obstacle and maneuvers so effortlessly at each battle thrown his direction.

He has better vision, clarity about the past, and, more importantly, his reactions. I have better understanding as to the love I felt was missing.

Truth be told, the only love I ever needed was always by my side as God so loved the world, He gave His only begotten son. Since I struggle with my spiritual beliefs due to my own insecurities and learned behaviors, I found Him to ultimately blame for the direction of my life. A life that tailed in a direction farther from Him, so in my head, my sin became my truth and love as I knew it was in the form of sin after sin as I chased the wrong love.

I spent many years of my entire life expecting a uniquely different outcome due my ignorance and lack of understanding that when you have love in a supreme fashion, life's love, as we know it in human form, well, it's inevitably easier to live with it, and all things fall into place after that fact. This is an internal battle with my current circumstances and mental shifting, so to speak, as I grow into another version of myself, a better version of the man I was at one time and ultimately the best version as the man God created me to be. A version that is grateful to have the small amount of life I have as I find humble is a scary place to sit, but to give is often the gift planted for your growth to bear the fruit of maturity in blessing as you guide from your history and place those past burdens inside a burning bush to allow the escape of the wrongs of life, which in turn allow all of you as you stand to be seen from the distance in the future.

To go back a bit and reflect, I want to take you through my mindset as to what love looked like and how it became the root of my own evil. In my eyes, love was pain; it's the pain that pierces through your being after you give all of yourself to a cause or purpose or, worse off, in my case, specifically a person. It's the reality after you sacrifice it all for the end goal. You give up your entire life it may seem for love.

You place it all on the line in the human form for what you thought was your American dream; your spouse-to-be; dreams of a great big house with the fairy-tale white picket fence, dog, children, and the pursuit of genuine happiness together; or however you choose to box it up.

Then out of nowhere and in the blink of an eye or with the snap of a thumb and finger, like Thanos was playing a true role in my existence, you awake, and it is gone. Your fairy tale has been replaced with extreme levels of loneliness that never seem to subside.

You throw the red flag and ask for a replay, or toss in the white towel because the blows to your heart and soul are too heavy. You feel defeat is near as you get pummeled by the emotions attached to its levels of intense burn that don't seem to play fair. You mentally play back memory tapes, and you see her walking ever so calmly toward you.

She enters the room fresh off her return from a visit home, right before deployment overseas for two years, and she ask you out the blue with a straight face, "LeRon, can I ask you something? Do you think we could be friends if we aren't a couple?"

These will forever be the words that started the change in my entire world from what I knew it to be; more importantly, they were the force behind my extreme emotional breakdown and heartache to come as I now felt I had not a reason to live another day more. And this was supposed to be *love*!

Do you think we could be friends if we aren't a couple?

Did I really just hear this. Are you kidding me? I almost lost everything inside me and wondered what in the world made her ask me this, at this moment and at this time. What was it that crossed her mind and made this the perfect opportunity to have this intense of a conversation?

Because of my guilt, I wondered immediately, was it another guy? I had not been perfect, but that was my secret. I had not been caught in a scandal, though I did have my skeletons. I thought I was doing myself a service in a sick and demented way by so-called getting it all out my system before a full-fledged commitment. I had never ever been single in my entire life. I met my son's mother when she was twelve years old and I was thirteen. We got married at eighteen, and I was nineteen, and I was legally tied in marriage, not monogamy, my entire adult life.

This by any means is not a cry for understanding from you and your judgment. I am judged by one, and that is God, so it's okay. Go ahead and have your thoughts, but honestly recall some of the trials I experienced by this time in life with social acceptance, premature sexual experiences, unwanted physical activity, acceptance. And other mentally challenging obstacles along with all the inner-city normal.

Truth be told, four years prior, I asked her in the midst of my new legal separation if I could actually have a moment away from our situation to be single so that I could rid my demons and be who I knew I could be completely for her as a man. See, to be honest, I knew me, and I knew if I fell in love as I had, I would fall in real love like I did; I would push the limits. I would love to the max, so I really didn't want the normal activity to be in the way. I tell myself this now far after the fact, but my actions said otherwise.

I knew entirely by the time I committed in word to a ship with her, with my escape routes established already, I would use the same activities I had in my marriage as a crutch to prevent future heart-ache. I talked openly and often to her about my fears and want to not hurt her, and at the end of it all, she simply gave me a rebuttal. Her own ultimatum I was not willing to abide by completely.

In a harsh tone, she said, "Okay, do you, but don't think I am not going to do me, and oh yeah, by the way, don't think I am just going to be here when and if you decide to return." Do me? Well, for one, the suggestion of having a little space to gather yourself especially while life was in the spin cycle truly didn't and shouldn't ever insinuate doing anything. It should mean, "Hey, let's date, not creep. Let's be authentic, not fabricated off the tail end of my nuptials." I mean, yes, I had issues, a cheater by all means. I knew I was a sinner, and I told her my story, I watched the shows, and I recalled all my brokenhearted moments, and actually I didn't want to lose her how she got me—from another woman's bed.

My thoughts after her last word were simply, wow, what in the world am I to do now?

I felt backed into a corner as there wasn't a plan or script for this. I didn't have the backup or way forward for her response, and plus it didn't help the way I presented it either, jokingly talking about space which was the request and playfully adding in how I needed to legally get my extracurricular sex, so to speak, out the way so that I could be an honest man for her, and not in those words, if you get what I'm saying.

How is it I am expected to do something I have never done, without getting myself some sort of break to fix myself to ensure I was the right man for her in the long run was my thinking. I had never done this before, and my track record was inexplicably horrific. I really didn't want to repeat my behavior, and honestly, because of the love I already felt for her at the time, I really thought it would be an opportunity to prove it so. I would have legitimate space and not be living with her, and I could see if I would find business elsewhere or still long for her touch and tone and find myself so eager to simply drift back in to her arms after a month or maybe even a few weeks.

I truly wasn't looking for an all-out sex fest; I just needed clarity before commitment because I was tired of lying to myself and being a fool for fake love and not believing I would ever find real love in the eyes of God, yet she was my one. Truly I knew she had all I wanted.

Needless to say, I stayed, and though my local actions tailed to not. I found ways to meet my backdoor open policy throughout our relationship. So to digress, my mind next moved to how in the world, years after my request, can you just roll up and immediately decide all of a sudden you are ready to fall out of love with me, what did I do, what mistakes were made in such a short period of time that would make you throw away years and years of building together, and most importantly, why?

It was my norm to blame others in the past since that's what most cheaters do. I looked for the holes in her excuses. I was told I didn't commit fast enough, yet I committed, and not only that, but I committed to a lot of things I will speak on I'm sure another time. The end goal, well, I even eventually committed to children and the struggle of IVF as a man who had two adult children and no desire to have more until her request.

I verbally committed to matrimony and assumed that feeling was mutual. Come to find out it was one of her reasons for dissolving the relationship as she said I spoke too openly and loud about marriage without taking the steps to make it happen. Yeah, I did speak it as I wanted to speak it into existence, but really, I needed to make sure it was done correctly as we both didn't have the picturesque-type wedding in our earlier lives. I only wanted to make it special, so when she was looking back on the journey, it would be one that was memorable and that of those we often watched from afar. Time was not of the essence and didn't play in my favor even after two rings and several shed tears.

Her next reason was her backup line.

After everything, she stated that I didn't support her new career as a naval officer since I said I didn't want to do thirty years in the Navy, when what I meant was I didn't want to share my future wife with the military full time forever since I personally knew how things happened and the numerous pitfalls with love and life due the militaries non-warming way of dissecting happy homes for moments to be.

Was it my own insecurities since I was the product of the Navy and its unique way to partner two individuals for a six-plus so or more relationship outside their norm? Was it the fact that I now was playing the role of my ex-wife and being forced to sit at home while my counterpart was out on another mission doing her job and my past was here haunting me? It was front and center giving me the illusion that because I was so much of a bad steward that it was time that karma played a game of truth or dare in my head while she was away.

Was it me fearful that my antics wouldn't stop and I would continue to be as disrespectful as I ever had been for my own selfish reason? No matter how its boxed up inside, it was the same old stench that was always there, and it was me bringing along all my insecurities from childhood and beyond.

It was my life excuses and imposter role coming to the forefront, and without the control over things I normally had, I was forced to reconcile with my own inability to simply trust the process and believe in it, for love, if it is what it's to be, it would be strong enough to weather any storm.

The problem is we both were missing a very important ingredient. We had zero relationship with God, individually or as a unit.

I now know I was destined for continued destruction, for I had no spiritual basis, no godly assistance; there wasn't anything related to His blessing anywhere in our lives.

I knew it, she knew it, and yet we still never acted. We even talked about finding a church, but in between house parties, frequent monthly travels, her job, and me starting a business while in school, we found it easy to put God on the back burner. Mistake number one. Trying to find peace, I would say to myself, *Look at how we came to be as a couple.* It was one of those unique moments the military places you in while vulnerable, and the lesson is learned that fast, and I didn't want to be another story told on smoke decks and other platforms during deployment about a past.

I lost sanity and all control; I had zero plan nor prep for this move; it was love's ultimate checkmate. I was loved and overtly emotional in a negative way because in those words sat my future as I saw it, and all I worked for in my eyes was now gone. I knew it was over, but I bandaged my feelings and played the role of the victim, for I felt she was doing to me what she did to the prior, and now it was her way of selfishly attempting to move on and leave me to the wayside without much damage.

The way men feel matter too!

Black men are so misunderstood, I think, we get tossed and forgotten as easy as we are picked up like strays because it is normalized in our culture unlike therapy, help, and counsel.

I blame us for not seeking the proper help to fix past hurts, but I also wonder if the nights of conversation and opening up really went unheard. I wonder if she felt I needed zero fixing, and if not, what was wrong then? I don't believe she took into account the sacrifice made to simply be by her side, the sacrifice it took to play my role in her newfound success and the attempts to cater to one who actually helped save me as a man after many failed attempts at life. The hurt lingers because I already had a picture in mind as to what the years in advance looked like; this was devastating. She eventually said she wanted no more to do with me, and to make it worse, without clear and concise reasoning.

This is love! Really, I mean, is this love?

Is love this emptiness and incompletion you live with, leaving you to feel less than and as if you were simply tossed aside like a mangled rag no longer needed for why it was originally purchased? Or is it the fact that you were a shell of a man still leaving back doors open for possibilities and escape routes for these moments, in case you needed to have reason. I was not or never have been perfect, and my sins are all in forefront as I could not escape the life I have known for years.

Even as I write this, I find it so hypocritical to be upset with her for her decision because I didn't get caught or because I didn't do as much to protect my own personal interest. The fact was I did have holes in my armor, and I was living as a man that was not right to be blessed to be with her, for I was who I was. A long-time cheater who knew nothing about the fruit that monogamy is but the escape that another was, regardless of if I was married or in a relationship.

Cheating is entertaining another person however you do it when its emotion-driven and the other person is not the one you chose to commit yourself to. Place holders or possibilities, like I was holding my best spades hand, just waiting to be asked what was my bid by my partners in crime.

I was guilty as charged, so I am slowly learning to accept the fact that I loved and lost, but regardless it was my fault.

Selfishly I watch TV shows and find momentary happiness in knowing I am not alone in my misery. The TV shows and online breakups of men and women going through so many similar fights with love and lust, cheating and divorce, monogamy and infidelity. I say to myself, *You are not alone.*

This lapse in judgment is baffled by the fact I am currently without an address, or let me correct myself: I am living in an RV, and though I find the satisfaction to be very small in nature and truly irrelevant, I get reminded that those on screen have resources to fall back on. I digress. Before jealousy gets involved, step back, reassess the view, and decide to leave well enough alone.

My battles are mine to own, and the travels of another don't intersect the lanes of life I'm in. We are all given a life, and we live it to the best of our abilities. The haves and have-nots don't justify the right or wrong, so for me to have reservations because one person battles easier or harder is not an option. I let it go for what it is before getting out of character, because dwelling on things I cannot control only creates a bigger obstacle for me to deal with, and that is personal failure which is outside the topic of my current struggles with love.

So to all who live and deal with the struggle, I hope that you have the time to find clarity and peace. I hope you get the chance to sit and reflect on what you have invested and what you possibly stand to lose. Love doesn't take into account your worth or your lack. It doesn't see the kids or the material possessions. It doesn't know your current place in life or society. Love comes to do what it does: it turns the party up or shuts the party down; there is no in-between cause love doesn't cost a thing, but love will cost you everything! Just google it!

Pieces from My Past in the Mirror

nger mounts; tears rain down like water from a showerhead—
that's where I often cried at that time. A place where I could
simply mask the picture of hurt I was forced to endure, normally
alone; I dealt and had no way of cutting it off. You lie down, and you
sit; you feel miserable looking for excuses and reasons to make you
feel good enough to press on.

You began lying to yourself to make it better, and the layers peel
themselves back in bits without clarity. You mask the reality that it's
over. You hope and have faith that this grasp you had on what your
version of it was, that this person will eventually reach out because it
was real and true, it wasn't a dream nor time wasted; it was real, so I
tell myself, and you await it to reach out and contact you and say I
miss you, I'm sorry, I love you; and each day goes on, and the more
days that pass, the more realistic it is that you aren't going back into
the arms of love like in the movies; it's not as jazzy as the chorus in
the songs, it isn't the picture-perfect fable from within the books, and
you are truly in the face of what love is.

It is at that point you can respect it and for small moments
understand what it is and what It was like. This totality is the shock
moment that you face, and now you look to find someone, something, anything to blame for the reason you are where you are currently. The truth is you find yourself looking at you, your actions,
your reactions, the life after, the drama, the finger-pointing and raised
voices, the ugly text and email confrontations from miles apart, and
your dead-end moments cause you to wrestle with the fact that you
probably were never equal in it.

The fact that one could move on so effortlessly speaks a different volume, and it is amplified in real time. How could someone in love simply forget, tossing aside your dreams of forever just because? Followed by, how could someone in love always have someone else awaiting love, in the case you needed a way out?

Before leaving for the Navy, I watched my parents battle day in and day out with life and what I assumed was some sort of love. From what I gathered in my youngest of years of inquiry, it went a little something like this.

Step 1. You find love. So many stories are told of those first moments and the meetings in life we have. We are led somewhere or reach out to someone we make acquaintance, and boom! Love is in the atmosphere, or you are minding your own business, they pass by or speak randomly, and love, it just so happens to find you.

Step 2. You do what's necessary to have it and maintain it, and you live the best you can in it no matter what. You ride it out when it is real, for this is what forever is all about. You take the good, the bad, the long, the short, the stink, the fights, the sorrow, the healing, the hurt, the pain, but the love binds us, so we are one with it for life, so I assumed. As for my parents, I never heard them fight nor asked if they were in love truly as I grew. I actually believe that there was a lack of it or some sort of disconnect at times especially during the down times, which there were more to count than not. I believe that it was misused amongst them which began a cycle of lovelessness amongst myself, my sibling, and parents plus extended family as we grew without it a lot in a substantial form.

I think people assume because you're in a two-parent home and the outside is nicely manicured that their secrets and past transgressions aren't the demons sitting in the wake waiting to ravage the entire family. What once was the picture of black excellence in poverty became a daily struggle and a nightmare with fights to find the simplest forms of affection in a household where the children were left many times to fend for themselves.

Most often because the system which gave a black couple who knew nothing more than Mississippi and their small corners of freedom and small breaks in life before simply withdrawing the rug from under them with a cultural reminder of who they were. Living in a society where sundown truly meant being inside at sundown due the location of your existence and color of your skin. Equality, I laugh every time I consider that word and this country. Equal (sighs), how that was never a word used properly in my part of town. Equality is a mental roadblock in the culture. It probably played as much of a role in my life in its lack as love did.

The lack of being equal in a time when stereotypes came multi-directional, swift, and in several forms. I believe it's the lack of basic equality that has tarnished my skill sets and limited my interactions in particular places just as love and its misuse of it did.

I became a serial impostor to fit in equally amongst those I never would have sat in rooms with had I not joined the service and found accomplishment. I had to become a chameleon of the sorts and find basic ways to fit my real life and my fake lives all into one circumference so they would roll in unison as expected with flaws and all.

The role of a fake, so to speak, is how I equate it.

We all have it and are all guilty of it; I just now admit to it. But like so many of my actions, I kept this secluded because the world would assess labels and denounce actions without knowing the reason, just as the world so coldly does.

I wasn't promoting fake, but just as when the bill collector called and I changed the tone in my voice, I would use a separate tone when speaking to the captain and another when talking to a female friend and another to my homies and another with the wife and so on and so forth. Little do we all know, eventually, out of habit, we take these acts on as traits, and characters begin to form. Eventually you have multiple personalities or characters at a minimum living inside our heads, all on standby for the call to duty when needed.

This is why I say we should not disrespect those who are different, those who make decisions for their way of life, those with mental illness, etc. since I feel we all suffer; some happen to suffer more serious in episode than others, and some will never be honest about it, but we all have been someone else before in our lives.

A certified impostor, a fake, a fraud, and yet we all keep it one hundred. Yeah, okay, one hundred, I hear you talking. As a child you don't understand these things, but with a sick mother who often had mental health breakdowns, you learn that the love that you were missing was taken. It was snatched because society forced two broken adults to manage a household the best they could, left to rely on faith and their strong belief system behind God, Jesus Christ, and the Holy Spirit.

That belief, as I sit and beg Jesus to help save my soul and preserve what's left of my mind, is the same one that I was forced to figure out all while blaming God for my youthful adversities.

Often, I wondered why I had been given such despair. If I was learning the speeches and participating in the plays, I prayed and joined the choir, I was mischievous, yet what child isn't? I was confused, and my anger and resentment turned into an onslaught against the place my parents forced me to attend usually without my vote Sunday to Sunday.

The church. With regards to church and service, the older I got, the worse my attitude got. I became bitter and loveless, for I didn't understand. I didn't see other kids in my class screaming about church at school or talking about how much time they spent reading the Bible. Never once did I hear my counterparts sing praises to Christ for all the material possessions they acquired. I was shown the hustle and grind of life and how to get it out of the mud. This was in the culture a real thing.

I never associated any of the immediate happiness I have seen in the streets with church and the knowledge of blessing if the hood chicks seemed happy in their roles and the dope boys got the daily attention; how in the world would God allow that to happen and them be the role models I have in life?

I never heard the playas and gang members scream about their personal enjoyment in it; the civic leaders and teachers never spoke to it. The cops and other city officials didn't place much importance on it, so why was I being forced to partake? Every Monday at school there were conversations about the malls, video games, skate rinks, the park hanging out, and spending the night with each other.

Those grew into talks about who was sleeping with whom and what drugs were being done or sold. Whose mamma was sleeping with whose pop and where the next party was going to be held. Who had the latest fashion and who was going to get beat up after school.

I always avoided altercations. I wasn't much of a fighter; I was a slick talker though. I stayed out the way, knowing the conversations above were not at first mine but were a lot soon to be my same conversation points. In my head, the other kids were living high on the hog and had all the so-called good things in life. Here I am doing what God says and wearing hand-me-down clothes from the same church I attended and probably clothes the same aged church kids who attended wore.

The fact I knew my parents tithed all their little money to the church to be left to struggle killed my spirits as I would wonder why this was my blessing, why can't my parents afford anything? Yeah, me, Mr. Materialistic as an adult now, go figure, and I wonder why. Well, it's because I wore those second-hand clothes, yes indeed I did, and I cut the tags and switched the symbols; I was a Monday-Wednesday-Friday-outfit kind of kid.

Needless to say, that same spirituality I lean back on even though it was not my strong suit as an adult was the concrete foundation and must be the only reason I am still here with the weight of sins I carry, and I can only believe my parents as well. It has to be why they are both still alive. Those long nights of prayer and consistency throughout turmoil in the church. The purity in belief that God has and will continue to show them favor due His grace and mercy, this I personally believe wholeheartedly.

After that detour in script, let's journey back into phase.

My point is that love, well, honestly, I just figured you grab it, and when you really find it, it's supposed to just work, like there's this supreme blessing from above, overseeing the entire thing, walking alongside your sinful journey, ensuring even through darkness you always have some form of it.

I understood what sin was. I also understood why Jesus died on the cross and what the so-called ways to being a Christian properly were. At least I assumed I did. I had never been an adult in love, and the people I saw and the things I knew surely didn't always mirror the books of the Bible, prayers, and scriptures the deacons quoted as to what it meant to be Christian.

What I saw was what life was like as an adult. I mean grown folk stuff I overheard it, I have seen it, I listened to it and soaked it all in, and all too many times a young child was subject to the vices of man and woman way too early in life.

I never experienced real faith and godliness growing up at least. I don't believe outside of when at a young age the pastor Rev. Dr. Donald Hunter, after a sermon, opened the doors of the church and asked if anyone wanted to come and give themselves to Christ. I don't recall my emotions of the moment or my feelings exactly, but I do remember walking toward the center of the front near the pulpit as he yelled out come on down if you want to be saved and live along with Christ come to the front.

Come and cleanse yourself and save your soul and live with God as one, in a Christ-like manner, or something to that effect. It was here I found myself moved to walk like Christ, and at this moment, I was all in. There isn't a turning around or do-over. Once you got up and proceeded to walk toward Christ, it was that moment of commitment the challenges begin in my eyes.

This is when life starts to happen, and I personally believe we do not take this moment as serious as God does. It is here where I believe a personal relationship and bond is started like blood brothers pricking their finger and mixing their blood in an attempt to create a unison that means forever. The only issue is when you are a child, you really do not understand the severity of such callings or the effort one must put into it and not just the act of it to create the lifelong bond with God that is necessary to actually walk properly alongside Him in life.

It was one of the more memorable times in church, and I recall the happiness on my parents' face as this was one moment that didn't involve them forcing me to do anything. I simply felt moved to get up and make my love for Him known and in front of the entire church. That was New Sunny Mount Missionary Baptist Church. This was the very place I made my commitment to Christ.

This was a place that afforded me several life lessons and assisted me with employment as a sixteen-year-old father, same place the minister would play a pivotal role in salvaging my life after a miscued drug deal forced me to join the military, and the same place that I eventually would commit some of my most disrespectful acts at as well.

My family was very spiritual; they were the bookends that held buckets of the sacred Holy Ghost, I believed. It was in their veins. I often wondered if it was because of their past lives in the deep South. Growing up in Mississippi during a time when most only had faith that life had more to offer.

America has always forced dark-complected people to pray harder and believe that in order to make it, divine intervention was necessary. They believed in the extraordinary, but me, I was broken from birth, so my belief came with questions. I didn't have that feeling or that tingle. I think, because of numerous life obstacles, I was numb to the possibility that God even knew I existed, let alone cared about the outcomes of my subpar living conditions, let alone my struggles.

Daily I dealt with real life problems. I didn't have the script on how to use my faith when I needed it most. There were several conflicts and road blocks I met as a child followed by teenage confrontations with death, robberies, drug dealing, and avoiding gang life, all while fathering a child at sixteen.

My immediate priorities were established. I lacked severely in my faith, always finding dead ends in life. My current life obstacles are a reflection of who I was. More knowledgeable about the subject my ignorance turns to anger as day in and day out I am reminded of why I am not in control of my life. I am shown that the gift is simply that and accomplishing greater is a lifelong art that you hope to find an end to so that you can just live and do your part.

Constantly shown what a good loving life could look like via artistic works to only fall into a bleak reality of what it is for myself, as I sit, forces me to believe that faith, though constant, does have its limits as you await your next or better.

I am a work in progress, a man broken over forty-eight years of living, damaged and taken advantage of, and this faith is supposed to be my lifeline as if it is the oxygen necessary for my every breath.

Faith. Faith, I will get a break and make better of myself in life. Faith that I too can have opportunity in a country that doesn't understand oppression is built into the lines of how I am treated, regardless the fact I sacrificed twenty-six years of my life. A country that used me up and sent me home just as broken as the day I offered my services. Faith that I am heard and can create change, that I too have a voice and can be heard over everyone else who feels they deserve.

I awake each day angrier than the last, but I am grateful in my own way that I do, for I know my complaints are heard and my life can be taken just as fast as it was given, yet to live without living is no life. I do believe God knows my heart like He knows I kept taking shortcuts vice the long routes to save time or face. Maybe this is forced comprehension since I was shortchanging spirituality for brief celebrity in an over-glamourized social life. We all chase something. Maybe this was my time-out to regroup before my opportunity was presented since I have been chasing everything but a relationship with him.

Break: emotional minute needed for clarity.

Driving Toward Safe
(poem)

What forces you to find the inner strength
to go on day in and day out when you are at your
last in life.

Those times when you feel that you have
zero left inside to give, not only to others but to
yourself.

When you find yourself being drained
by forces that are unseen and you have not the
proper tools to combat the energy amongst you.

You find your CenterPoint is blurred by the
light of your future.

Your question, you hope is answered at the end of the tunnel, or is it because the future is uncertain, so, you keep a positive attitude as the books you read say to do.

The reality is, it feels so indifferent.

Indifferent because you live in what is real and daydreams only seem to show their faces in the dark while you sleep as nightmares.

You listen to many who achieve forms of happy, a shame covers your spirit because you once felt their version of emotion.

In regression, you sit engulfed in a roller coaster of feelings while forced to visualize the lack and current state of your affairs while they speak on their storms and the famed ends of rainbows you currently search for.

The happiness at the ends of tunnels that are ongoing in your path never appear.

No option to turn left or right.

You see the sign, last stop before tunnel, do you have enough gas, who knows, for you feel drained and have given years of your all, now your cups are about dry.

You pray that you can make it.

Yesterday though bleak at best gave you hope so you push the limit and believe the other side is around the corner and you press on.

Inside of your thoughts, years of fear and uncertainty emerge so you brace yourself for the obstacles that may appear.

You enter the tunnel with pure intentions, you've traveled these roads before and the other side, well, we know all roads lead somewhere; the problem is the road untraveled, where will it lead.

Blindfolded in the journey, confused at your ability to focus on your path daily you find your talents jumbled amongst each other without any of them fighting for separation, so discouragement is in the passenger seat.

Buckled in for the ride, discouragement ensures they play the tunes of the life journey you traveled, loud and piercing are the melodies and basslines.

Song after song, your fails on repeat, stained with numerous faces is your memory.

These are the faces of old accomplices not friends for that word holds no weight in your vocabulary anymore as they have revealed their true intentions in being.

You stare in between the agony and eventually the emotions overtake your soul as each word presses against your chest in an attempt to make you suffocate.

Who once was riding in silence alone is now alone, with others who seem to always find themselves around, not to support or uplift but to ensure that you know who you were and why they are.

Passenger side rear, Depression sits at attention as you gaze up in the rearview mirror and you wonder who invited you on this ride.

Depression always seems to have an invite when your emotional state is uneasy, and you are vulnerable.

It's a freeloader and likes to carpool without even caring the route or final destination.

Depression believes it's helping to navigate life but it's really sending you through a maze, left to wonder who told you about this ride in the first place.

Must've been those old so-called friends again I guess, WOW!

You look at the walls in the tunnel, dimly lit are the overhead lights concentrating on the road as the walls swish one by one, like flashes from blank canvases and you start to see pictures, snapshots of places, and faces.

Subtle memories of where you've come from, and depression is excited like it's a trip down memory lane.

You try to refrain from arguing with your depression and find out they talk with others who are riding.

Anxiety and adjustment disorder find themselves seated in back as well discussing things about the day ahead and what's planned.

The rearview mirror is empty, and you feel the physical detachment from society the deeper that you ride into the darkness of the tunnel and yet your passengers are overwhelmingly excited, and all seem to be enjoying the trip into the past.

You tug at your waist to make sure your buckled in because anxiety keeps kicking the back of your seat like a child looking for attention when being ignored.

You fail to adjust in comfort so now the disorder in the vehicle is pushing you to panic wondering where it all went wrong.

Are you crazy, is this disability going to cause a 1-person accident, no traffic in a tunnel fatality of the sort?

You focus, think about it.

You streamlined your end goals; you had a life plan, you made bad decisions, and dealt with the consequence but the mission is not your own scripting it seems.

Is there something you've missed, is there a destination unknown.

You left all you knew to venture off into a world without a path and the baggage you do have is cumulative.

Reality is, you harbor emotions that seem to never allow you to release the troubles you try now to avoid and the ugly of life haunts you.

You set the cruise control and coast blindly into whatever is in store.

You hear the storm outside the tunnel loud and clear independent of the music your co-passenger plays on repeat, the twist and turns of the tunnel are rapidly shifting, your GPS is enabled but dysfunctional because of your location inside of yourself.

The tunnel narrows and the lanes tighten, your fears are now along for the haul, what did you do to deserve this pain, why me, why now you think; inhale slowly and exhale with meaning, just breathe.

This is routine behavior, you slam on the brakes, and slowly regroup before shock remembering that you are deep inside the tunnel.

Now you find the energy to drive on.

You have no option but to move forward, you're in a tunnel and there's no turning back at this point.

Day in and day out, lights on lights off, knowing that ahead is uncertain but optimistic is your mindset because of the stories of hope you believe in.

There are so many moments throughout each day where I feel that I have zero left to give, all while things are steadily being tossed at me.

After hours of driving up life's hills, through all its valleys, the highways, overpasses, city streets, and alleys, it's the tunnels that seem to push you the hardest.

Your passengers, still in tow but are now eerily silent, I reflect and see light.

Though it is vague in sight I do believe there is a chance this may soon be it.

Soon I will see opportunity to be free and alive once again to live out life without the tunnels of despair and moments of darkness.

My passengers finally removed and replaced once again with those who are support and the direction of my path guided so clearly that man-made tools are no longer needed to ensure I reach my final destination as GOD had the wheel the entire time.

Safe…

One day earlier this year I happened to be in such a state of turmoil I wondered what society thought of me.

I canvassed my social media accounts and searched different mediums to see what was available, about who I was in this cold world. Call it a gut-wrenching emotion or whatever, but the feeling made me look harder. I looked high and low online and eventually decided I would do what I saw my ex-fiancé do. I googled my name.

After typing into the search box, my name, LeRon Robinson, a ton of online websites popped up with claims to have tons of so-called relevant information about me and who I was, all attached to a small fee.

My instincts said this couldn't be right, for I have had a somewhat normal way of life, so how could this much information be attached to my person?

I served twenty-six years in the United States Navy, was honorably discharged, and 100 percent disabled. I was a business management student at ECPI University and in tune with my courses and classes. We were fresh off a pandemic scare which shut the nation and world completely down, so there wasn't much moving around the years prior.

I had a ticket or two in the past, and that was about it, so what could be in a report under my name? My curious nature moved me to pay the fee to acquire my information, and I did. I moved forward onto a site in which I knew she used before, and I scrolled up and down the file.

Then as I scrolled, I started to see things I knew were not of my own works. The level of issues was grave. The things that were attached to my name were monstrous in nature. Who was this person they said that I was? I got angered and upset assuming that this was a fake or some conspiracy theory against me and why. Why would this type of information be placed under my name online, and the bigger issue was how?

Most individuals hop right online and search for information just as I had, and if one looked to inquire as to me and my character the easy way, a few clicks would have shown them that I was a man of unfit character, a drunk, a drug addict, and, worse, a pedophile.

This was a deafening blow to me and my current state of mind.

My fiancé was fighting me; my family was nowhere around; my friends were being pushed aside; and I was in a hole, alone to deal with this information and now scared, for I didn't know who saw these lies about me. I didn't know who else googled my name to see the lies.

The man who committed the crimes I researched him extensively and found he was born in the same city and grew up in the same county I did.

I never met the guy as he was years my senior, finding he was born in May some years prior. He lived near the junior high school I attended. This was mind-boggling how it was to be.

What was more confusing is how in the heck could he have found his way to Virginia Beach, Virginia. Of all the places to go, he found his way to the city where I lived and spent so much of my personal time. I found out that he was a career criminal and had several adverse issues on his record, and most of the latter were placed on me. His crimes were incorrectly placed on my public record which could be acquired for a fee.

I called the city of St. Louis and several of the courts in which he had a criminal record with for them all to run my information and reassure me that I was clear and nothing on file as I already knew the same, yet how could this negative info find its way onto my public profiles?

I researched more and found that the most horrific of charges, the rape, was performed by him while I was in the midst of advocating as the Sailor of the Year and in and out to sea as we were preparing for deployment.

I got highly upset because I was informed that there were no rules or guidelines for online companies and how they compile the information which is placed under your report.

Basically, it's like Wikipedia, and anyone can place anything they like without repercussion from the government into an online profile. I had not raped a fourteen-year-old girl. I knew this, but the people who may run across my profile, how would they know, how could they know this wasn't me?

I dug in deeper and searched harder to eventually find that this year, the man who committed these crimes, same name, different middle name, was arrested and sentenced to prison. He is currently in prison serving time for the crimes aforementioned in a Kansas prison where I believe he rightfully deserves to be for the crimes he committed.

The sad part is the profile of a criminal who was rightfully charged and convicted, I assume, is placed under that of a free and innocent man. Why? I cannot answer you this. I cannot get answers and cannot get correction. I am simply subject to the ugliness of the world and how society has the ability to place judgment on man as if they were the God I serve.

This compacted amongst the rest of my current trials, and personal tribulations were pressing me to a state of dismay I am glad I didn't fall victim to. I wrestled up the energy to find security in knowing my truth and knowing my life was not the picture of hell placed online in the public's eye but that there was a way forward.

I suppressed the emotions, for this incident, though troubling and grave, didn't amount to the hurt and pain I felt as love was lost.

I wondered if she had done the same and looked up my name. I wonder if she saw that this was on my public file as I knew she searched others before. Maybe she looked me up and seen the ugliness that he was, and without question, this information made her flee from who she saw me as.

She had lay in bed with a cheater, yes, but not the person the internet shown me to be. I was a cheat and not a monster. Maybe she looked me up and felt I was a man less worthy to be in her life forever, and her way out was to simply love me from a distance.

The acts were from years prior our meeting, and maybe she assumed that this was me, but she knew me; she knew my character. Why wouldn't she ask me was my reasoning.

Back into my shell of hurt and despair as the analogy of maybe fixing a flaw is not one, I believe, would bring me any conclusion worth a happy end. This happened and ruined my name; she happened, and I ruined my life. I am permanently in my eyes left to lose on both accounts without a way forward. I am left to read Bible verses and sift through scripture after scripture in hopes of salvaging peace.

I try daily to find soft spots in the word to bring me a since of serenity vetting my ongoing way of life looking for small gleams of light in the darkness, but I am left each time in turmoil, questioning more than I simply allow myself to just be in the moments. I scan so much of the word and have found that accepting situations for what they are is frightening.

I find that accepting this as my way forward or trials of life is hard because I don't see the good in so much bad being subject to my way of living daily. What is to come from the rounds and rounds of pain? The current state of emergency I sit in goes unheard as another holiday arrives, and I am alone and feeling tormented by the hours, days, weeks, and months past. I give in and simply say I cannot control the things which aren't to be, so I let go and let *God*.

Excuse my ramblings. Those are for another passage maybe one day I will pen and let you in on. After that brief reflection, I fall back into my reality, and it is here I sit alone. I find myself alone in a twenty-foot travel trailer with a Yorkie, me crying off and on over a love I believe at times never was supposed to be.

The pain is extremely heavy, but I continue to carry its weight day in and day out, step after step, tear after tear, knowing I only ever wanted her for a lifetime, to laugh with and care for as I often did.

That person you see yourself playfully growing old with as you both find maturity. I guess I was not her love, not enough love; she lacked love or found excuses with love.

Maybe it was my plots around love or mishandling of her love, who knows, as she was nine years my junior and still in search of so much more in life after she divorced from an abusive love prior to our meeting.

Still, I wonder after and in between each sniffle, did she have a real emotion of the same tone, at the same time, or was I the perfect placeholder until her real love appeared and took her hand into the next chapter of her life, while I bask in the memory of wishing I simply had someone to wash my back?

From birth you are reaching and asking to be guided so that you face zero pain in your ignorance about life and all the forthcoming obstacles you will face. Everything you know eventually is something that is taught to you, driven into you as an ethic, moral, or standard of living, learning right from wrong, how to or how not to.

We are all, in some format, given instructions on how to live and directions as to do so, but where were the blueprints on what to love, why you should love, and, most importantly, how? When can you or when is it safe to love, when should you start loving, where are you to love, and most importantly, who should you love?

Since the word is never given fair context, you grow to assume song lyrics, movie scripts, and daily visuals are your blueprint, when all in all you have never really been trained on exactly the truth of love and what it should be.

Love for me was always attached to something dark or someone leaving me in a darkened state. It was not the beauty we visualize among flowers and behind melodic tunes. It was associated with an eventual pain. There was always the existence of hurt. Knowing that eventually, because I love, soon, in due time, I would suffer and feel the hurt associated with giving away pieces of mine without a future attached to nurture it properly. See, that's what my past showed me.

It is the culmination of all the faults I look back on and analyze after each fact of it while wondering what happened or derailed my plans for it. Any person who attaches a preconceived notion to it is destined to never experience it truthfully until the pain you never expect arrives, then you finally have confirmation that you were in it.

By that time, most likely and typically, especially in my case, it's too late. The experience is all over, and you find fault in it as you failed once again. My ignorance became my direction, and comfort was normalizing the pain I expected it to bring.

Because of my basic comprehension skills, I had a generic understanding of love. My issue was I didn't have the proper direction and/or instruction as to how real-life emotions tied to the word, so I only had life's daily struggle to associate with it.

I assumed some of us get lucky as if we guessed the right lottery numbers at the right time and get each one perfectly aligned with another person as they seem to have selected the same. You meet, there's a life alignment, and love simply clicks. It's as defined by the stars to be. Real talk, for now, my life hasn't been scripted as such. My life has attached so much pain, hurt, regret, and tears to the word that when it's felt, the fears are face front. The negative assumptions are through and through, to be assessed as real because it's only a matter of time before this supposed beauty called love will be its alter egos: pain, hurt, and tears.

Where did my instructions come from? Where did I get these directions?

As stated earlier, I was raised in a two-parent household. I never heard my parents argue much or disagree. See, they were old-school Mississippians, products of the struggle, and had large families. Were they loved growing up? I wondered. How did this work? Were my parents taught love's role? The "How to Love," in Lil Wayne's voice. Were they given the secret guide and even more? If they were, amongst the list of things they placed emphasis on to teach as parents, why didn't anyone ever share the blueprint? Especially if they knew that love's the one thing needed to survive that you can't buy and possess without properly acquiring it. If it's so necessary for our life to have, shouldn't they have forewarned me about its good, its bad, and all its worth?

Where were the stories about how they saw it in life and all I should look out for, what I should expect to feel when it's real, and what it should look like when it's true? Even if the only examples were from their life experiences, why did they never do what loving parents I assume we're supposed to do and inform to protect someone they love?

Forty-eight years later I sit in love with the pain I currently hold, knowing I found it and lost it. Maybe I blame them as part of my own life struggles, reflecting on how often they laughed with her as if it was plotted all along my downfall. Is this real, or are these paranoid distractions since my current problems are face forward? Maybe as I watch them struggle to live and hold favor with each other after years of being married, I hold them accountable for my current lack of the thing they claim to have.

I watch others cheer, support, and show love to those they choose when the success and achievement is readily accessible. As if the love is multidirectional because you feel all parties played a part. But who is there in pain when love fails? Why don't those who didn't give you the right tools cry and hurt equally as you sit and often suffer alone?

Born in Milwaukee, Wisconsin, I was told I may just have been the cleanest child on my block as I was my mother's first living child, something I just found out myself (hmmm). Another story for another day from an ongoing list of new details I continue to dig up under my queries.

My father told me that often as a toddler I would be outside playing in the world, and my mom, this brand-new mother who was in the midst of tackling life challenges and all she didn't know on the fly, would chase behind me with a rag to clean the dirt and accumulation of fun I would have on me. Hearing this from my father, I immediately associated her actions with love. I felt the fact she didn't want me to look dirty, feel dirty, be dirty, didn't want me to hurt or be in trouble was love. Love, well, yes, it is and was, but the issues to me were much deeper. As you grow, it is different, and the love you once pieced together transitions into a different form without explanation.

You awaken, and eventually that version is extremely shifted, and you are now expected to hold your own in life and in love. It is expressed in difference by the owner or supplier. Now how it's associated in use, meaning the owner or giver of it, may manipulate it as fit. This is a gruesome truth you have zero control over.

You learn to move on accepting what is given. You have no control over what they may believe is enough as it is equated by that person. This means love has layers, love is needed by all, but how much or little? How is it displayed? Is it the same for all who receive it? Why can it be given and taken away?

This was the beginning of numerous hard lessons I would learn about this word which drove me to not fully be able to properly give it nor receive it. As I grew to protect myself from love by any means necessary, I would eventually sparingly give it honestly, but I reverted back to my normal protective ways which ultimately destroyed it once I believe I had it properly. How do I know?

Well, my first critical mistake was still not establishing a relationship with God once I knew the feelings I felt. Instead of finding God, I placed all my securities in her. I thought that I had finally found a person I could trust in my nakedness to consistently wash my back. I found someone who, in my time of need, I could call to and not feel ashamed to say I need help. I not only need help but choose you to help wash the hurt, pain, trauma, despair, dirt, and etcetera from my back. I go through the motions, at the moment without instruction; I dread how my own actions sent that love away.

The fact I sent love possibly into another's arms, another place, or simply pushed her back into her darkness to ask about love from her own angle or view in life. To have her wish someone gave her direction, for all she saw was an abundance of broken promises from a father who was an alcoholic and never there.

She saw the extra her mother was forced to do alone, and that helped give her substance of life's grandeur, I am sure. She often acquired slight glimpses as most children of color do because of an empty home due economic struggle, single-parent households, the allure of the streets, incarceration, or whatever else the government could throw a minority's way. Maybe the only true version of what love was in her eyes came from that of her beloved grandparents.

As my parents were to me, so to her were they. They happen to be that lottery ticket in her eyes. They showed her what it was to love and be loved. She knew its emotion and external view, but she never was gifted the blueprint. She was sentenced into a world where a single mother of three was forced to awake before five to catch rides or buses and sometimes was afforded the luck to drive to work to provide. So now who teaches her how to love, or if it's even worth the time since her pictures like mines weren't properly painted?

How could two people be expected to follow the dream when neither of them had any real expectations to outlast the fears they accumulated prior their meeting? I remember washing her back. I can recall hearing her voice call out, "Hey, babe."

I'd scream back, "Yeah," from a short distance

"Would you come wash my back?"

Honestly, I was overjoyed. It felt personal. It was like a completion moment. And so I did, and I scrubbed and did a service.

I got all the confirmation I needed as to who I was at that moment in her world. I felt the request was the answer to the question, do you love me? I'm simple. And prematurely created a picture of completion prior in my head, I assume. See, I didn't need to say head on, "Do you love me anymore?" I attached the act to the word, which now gave me confirmation. Since I got my answer, I would then step into a stronger sense of it and ask her to do the same. This was her reciprocating gesture to complete the picture I painted in my thoughts.

Without hesitation, she did, over and over again. Taking my favorite soap and body wash, lathering it up and removing all the ugly from the place I could never properly reach. I would stand under the running water, feeling the troubles being washed away, all the while knowing I was safe and that I was loved. See, I created a direction; I created safety and instruction. So as life took its toll, no matter the obstacle, knowing that after it all, I had her to reciprocate love. And that small action was everything to me.

What I didn't know or want to believe was that you can't have the amazing feeling of love and still have personal protection or secret boundaries. In order to completely experience it properly, you either let all things go to focus on it, or you will only look into its pieces. You will save space for the what-ifs and maybes. And those are the same cracks that will eventually kill the happy you strive for.

You will go from knowing your back is good to hoping. Then to wanting, into wishing, ending up needing. And by that time, it's all a blur; memories come into focus daily.

You try to walk through the fire alone, but it's hot, and you feel deserted. No matter how you try, you can't reach the same space as she could reach. You bend and you contort, but that middle spot you can't reach it alone. So you quit, and you sit in the fact that damn, maybe I was in real love. Maybe my pain and prior ignorance, my mistakes and poor judgment ruined my chance at the picture I saw of it.

The melodic sounds sang about it. Maybe I had my numbers aligned and couldn't cash my ticket in. It's not as simple as it seems. See, there had to be a reason. The wall, to escape if needed, was built on purpose. And it was because love could never be understood.

You have spent your entire life looking for it not knowing its face; you didn't know its color or shape; you couldn't smell it from a distance; and the times you gave in and assumed it was there, life altered your view. It is then you're reminded of your truth. You are forced to relive pain and personal drama, to look old fears up like exes, and you think of how that felt, how it hurt.

You hear that, subtle; I love you in many different voices and wonder where they all are now. You see the faces, remember the nights you felt their skin, and recall their deep connections. You often play the memories over and over, knowing the whos but never having an end. It only ends, and when it does, you get angry, upset, and simply repeat.

Having a hard time moving forward like normal, you understand its difference; this was unique. She was special and worth the hurt in a sense. This was me finally walking out my life's storm into a chance at happy, and I did the one thing I wish I hadn't via my ignorance. I brought my bags of safety with me.

See, since I created my own toxic version of what love was to be, I had to ensure I wouldn't feel my past pain again. It was already killing me. I suffered through a marriage I now know I should have never created, but all in all, I did and damaged so many lives along that journey. My dysfunctions in life led to me never being single, yet living a full-fledged single life where I spent my days and nights looking for real love, wanting it the right way, not how I chose it unfortunately. I mean, I only wanted the right someone to wash my back.

Seconds feel like hours. Hours feel more like days, and you're forced to sit in silence, knowing you truly found what you thought was yours. Your opportunity to show all those old situations your true worth. That you were ready to love without the help from Nephew Tommy or the OWN network, you figured it all out on your own. That you could do it and not only do it but be proud you had taken the leap of faith, hoping you guessed correct.

You could finally throw in the towel and live the rest of your days out in bliss. But I have found we all don't get to the end of the coveted rainbow. We all don't feel the warmth of the secure space love supposedly brings. Honestly, I believe, like myself, the world is full of mes who were never properly given the correct tools on love. So we cross each other's paths, one number off never properly engaging out of fear from the last turmoil, scared to pass along any emotion amongst each other. We are life's love passers.

This leads me to another word I am learning slowly to accept in life, *hope*. You hope that it's right. You hope that it's real. You hope your feelings are mutual. Hope this is the last one. Hope you can make it work. Hope there is a place to build. Hope tomorrow comes. Hope these aren't distractions. Hope you can breathe in this forever. Hope you don't mess it up like the past. Hope it feels the same. Hope there is a future. Hope you can build this one better. Hope the word is real because I hoped I could get a backwash every night from her knowing that.

Hope was the string which held tons of pain secure since in my eyes we were in real love. My back, oh, how the dirt accumulates day in and day out while forced to look into the silhouettes of souls I tried to replace you with. The many strings which I kept attached, who so often praised my relationship, I feel preyed on it at the same time.

The fault was my own. It was me allowing past pain, hurt, and insecurities to keep back doors open for an expected eventual necessary retreat. My biggest flaw in life and safe space, the art of running and removal which shown I truly was not ready for this, not this feeling I would have to sit in once again but on a uniquely higher level.

I had been in love similar to this most recent chain of events but not to the level exactly. Many years earlier I left my family for what I believed was love and found myself shut down by her on day one of my arrival with gifts in hand because I listened to the lies told to me during our sexual exploits and bedroom tangles. She told me she loved me unconditionally and how we would be such a powerful couple and that our coexistence was possible time after time, except my family was the only thing in our way.

Crazy how this was what always determined my level of love. That said, it played on my psyche, and I thought about what had happened previously to us and the part I played in it all. Her words rang out like a bell since everything I wanted was placed a second time in my face, and I fell for it. I wasn't going to let it slip out of my hands. I was to finally be in a loving happy relationship with someone who cared for me the same.

I think from birth I was cursed; I also felt and feel I don't have real support from my extended family due to me being enlisted and away for thirty-plus years. The self-proclaimed black sheep always messing everything up and everyone along the way, it wasn't until my late thirties that I actually felt I was accomplishing things in life, but even then, I now realize these were simply ways I could stress that I wasn't a failure or the ugly kid from school with no childhood story of beauty and accomplishment.

I was placed in a very uncomfortable position where life was being taught to me in a way that was not of Christ, and the scars would remain embedded in my soul for years after. I still to this day do not understand completely what and why but know the episodes which took place during a summer visit to the south were not those which a child should be subject to. It is very confusing and still haunts my spirit as each day I blame my ills in life on a specific moment which molded my future forever. Flashes of erotic magazines found stashed in a location and reenacting the photos without understanding what was being done would create a trauma which still to this day has not been completely removed.

I was introduced to the devil's ills. For years I have chipped away at the memory of that time; the moments are vague. I have gut-wrenching flashes of the interactions and lots of confusion as to why me.

I guess I should submit and follow through. *Maybe this is love. Maybe this is how you are noticed.* Still I never got anywhere. I knew that feeling wasn't right; it wasn't what I saw on TV and who my parents were.

This led to early onset experimentation with females and exploiting the act of sex without any intent of love. I was vulnerable and hurt, and these feelings led to me searching for something. My challenge was not knowing that sex wasn't the answer because while searching, a loveless teen became a dad.

They say you understand love once you become a parent. Well, honestly, I didn't and became a father and still was confused about every single element of life as I was living it. Someone else controlled my dreams of happiness, I thought, and so I ended up a child fathering a child and forced myself to learn to love this child and my new circumstances.

I can't say from his birth I was in love with this child since the child was now restricting me from being one. Recall, I didn't know love, but I knew care, and I cared for my child, yet I blamed him and his mother for where I was in life at that moment. Honestly, I blamed them both for now keeping me from ever being anything else but what I was at that time.

A son bearing my name which I didn't even have input in. I was not even old enough to be in the delivery room as most fathers are. I had to sit in the waiting room and catch the first glimpse of my child through a plexiglass wall after he was placed in his holding bed after being born due my age. December 22, 1990, he was introduced into this world. A cold winter day I will never forget as it became the day his began and also the day I felt my life was now over before it was even to start. I would never fall in love in life or have the chance to find that person I could ask to wash my back.

Recently, I logged in to our modern-day dictionary (Google) and typed in, "How many times does a person fall in love in a lifetime?" Numerous articles and several other items were quickly populated and readily at my disposal. After scrolling up and down through the list, I think the answer to my question was answered by who had the biggest paycheck to the host. How eyebrow-raising, and to believe I spent my entire adult life banking on what Sir Google had to say, as we all do and many of you still do to this day. My online research generated the number four most often.

I looked deeper, and it stated the average was between 2 and 7, which I believe to be a lot more accurate because of society and many other things which have direct impact on our lives such as population, change in economics, and a want to readily find yourself in a loving situation.

Personally, I have found myself in several situations of the heart and the different times I placed myself out there in front left me in several entangled situations. You see what I did there?

Real talk, I spent my entire life trying to find real love, and I was a sucker for anyone who was willing to give me a shot. Not only was it because of my inferior social status growing up and lack of love as I thought from the inside. It was also a cry for help and a plea for normal. I found myself simply wanting to be what my parents were as a couple. The picture from the outside of perfect. Unfortunately for me the street usually found yellow tape wrapped around what was left of my heart, and rightfully so, because of the way I went about finding these intimate run-ins. I will not place childhood love in this equation.

I was undereducated socially and sure my mind truly had not developed properly to even understand what the values in a lifelong love would entail. Most of the love I found myself in as a youth was the typical superficial love. That of being appreciated at the moment until you were in the next person's eye.

Only thing was in my life growing up I never had the opportunity of a next. I had my son's mother, and having a child kept me out of the eyes of many others as I looked like a guy who was sexually active, and what kid wants to involve themselves with a kid who is already prematurely exploring with the taboo of sex and actually had a child before his driver's license ink dried?

I was living in an adult world, and this scared most females away from me, so I stuck it out most times with my son's mother. There wasn't a genuine love, like in love, but there was love, like, I have love, as she was primarily all I knew, and I felt like I owed her oftentimes because she did me a favor and gave me a chance. Honestly, we were two kids who didn't have any structure that found security in each other.

We did everything together to void the ills of the ugliness around our area. We went to different schools but lived in walking distance from each other which made a daily rendezvous possible. Her father was a fireman and often worked very long hours, so she had most of her time to herself as her older sister was already into real life, and her younger brother spent most his time with her mother while she was piecing her new life together.

This left ample opportunity for extracurricular activity, and due my inquisitive nature and need to reassure myself of things from my past, the opportunity to fall was presented, and as I said prior, it wasn't love but love for the like and the moment.

By this time in life, I was having sex like a full-fledged adult. Never given the talk from my father, heck, I barely ever saw him, as his routine was up at five, off to work, school after, and then church, and this was daily. I didn't see him, let alone ever have a conversation with him about life. My father might as well have been absent and removed from my existence.

I actually don't have many stories of things we even did together in my teenage years, to no fault of his own I now understand. The system gave him limited resources, and his wife was fighting a mental health battle I am sure neither of them were prepared to fight, so he worked and educated himself to make more money.

He was overlooked, year after year, for promotion, and he did this all while praying to get a break, I guess. I had a father in the house, yet he was never in the house or allowed to have a break to be one because the struggle in the system doesn't give you opportunity.

I do believe my father loves me, and I think he did the best he could, but I know that the faults of his upbringing showed in how he attempted to play his role in life. He was raised by the hand of a stern man who expected you to know things by watching, and this in turn played out in how he parented as well. The only issue is he was never around to watch, so the streets became my teacher. The streets showed me right from wrong. How-to guides were now given by life; it was all trial and error.

At the time I didn't know how to use a condom, let alone why they were so important to not only control reckless behavior but to prevent catastrophe from happening. The tapes I watched surely didn't promote the use of prophylactics.

As for my sexual actions with my ex, I was all in, and then real life happened. You learn being an adult isn't all it's cracked up to be especially when you're a kid yourself and already impoverished. It made life horrific to live; you feel you have zero way forward, so of course you find your way into the streets to try and make some sort of easy money for the now to keep up with what society says is popular not knowing that the lifestyle is just that—it is a lifestyle.

You learn most of the chasing of all that the style that supposedly offers for a greater tomorrow will only leave your life in shambles. Jail and my constant fear of death was a daily compromise as you learn the way of the streets especially when you had zero street in your body. A church kid turned street kid, how did that happen? Guess I have a means to another script, huh?

With all that being said, I never experienced real-type love growing up. I had not had access or real interactions which would have led me to it. The only other time I believe it may have existed, she left me for a classmate, and several years later she unfortunately passed. She was a beautiful person inside and out and chose me. If only for that brief moment before breaking my heart, I felt she had chosen me.

Her name was Sophia Washington. She was well dressed and unique in her look. Very quiet and softly pressed as she would enter a room and to me embody everything a future would look like. She had charisma and dreams of a better tomorrow, always looking at the positive in life. We never talked about sex or lust or love as our conversations were about the future and where we both hoped to be in life if we made it out of the city. We would hang out after school as most times I would ask to walk her to her house which was in a completely different direction yet worth the time.

There was never a rush into the adult world because honestly, I understood chivalry and the beauty of those gentleman-like actions, so there wasn't a need to rush things. I was actually okay with the process. She eventually broke up with me and decided to move on without a reason, clear-cut, and I was torn to pieces.

For a long time after that, I despised her new beau. I felt the school would glare and look at me snickering under their breath at me. Whispers of, "Ha-ha, yo chick left you," and, "He took your girl," and, "What is wrong with you? He took yo chick." This was depressing and, I believe, my first real battle with mental health to a significant degree. This wasn't about material or anything that could be bought or sold. There wasn't any change that could be made to replace the fact that I had her with me and now she is with him.

How do you get that through a young man's head who struggled with so much before he was even thirteen? This was my first real battle with the opposite sex, ugliness and neglect from my peers. If you have school-age children, I beg that you inquire. Find a way to get into their most secret of secret lives, not to create a line in the sand but to save them from destructive behavior in the case they do not know how to deal with the circumstances at such a young age. They will have a life full of obstacles to battle, and the least amount of luggage they carry forward in their heads on the journey, the more room they actually will have to enjoy what life is to live vice living life looking to love as I did.

My first love as a kid, her name was Sophia. Ironically the first person I fell in love with as an adult that carried the same name. I wonder if this was a message to be or if it was a curse, but unknowingly, I now sit and think of the irony.

At nineteen years of age, I met Sophia, a woman from a country town in Georgia who crept in and took my heart by surprise. Ironically, I currently sit in Georgia near her hometown. She was my first real introduction to what I believe love was to be. My first of all and the woman who opened up Pandora's box and gave it power over my life. I left that situation unwillingly due my young naval career which took me from Millington (Memphis), Tennessee, and sent me to California.

There in California I had a relationship with a female I met at the club. Though brief in nature, it gave me life while I was on the west coast. I thought I was good, but actually I was doing what I could to get over the love I thought I would never find again. I was extremely broken and began drinking alcohol daily to mask the memories of her. See, in those days, you were allowed to drink as long as you were on a military facility. You didn't have to be twenty-one years old, and since I had been an alcoholic prior my enlistment, it was simply legal for me to choose my drinks was all.

The situation was what I needed to fill my sexual needs, but there wasn't any substance as oftentimes I think I settled because she had wheels, and I could get around from point A to point B without having to catch the bus like normal since my car was home with my son's mother. Our relationship, to me, was the typical "use me for your needs and I'll use you for mine" type.

I was starting to get rooted in California and getting to know the streets and club scene finding my way around town and looking for female companionship when I got a call that said I wouldn't be in California much longer.

I eventually left and ended up in Virginia Beach, Virginia. Yep, I went from coast to coast in the matter of a few months. This is where the boy becomes a man. Virginia was a different place for me; it took time for me to get used to boots and shorts and the way they lived, but I acclimated quick and soon after had a squad. The military I found was different from how I grew up because no matter where you went, there were people to get to know as long as you had the right attitude; there was always someone looking for an associate. It was perfect for my persona because the lifestyle was unique.

Take people from all over America and give them a job and place them all over places around the States and give them time. This time would become my playground as I canvassed the routes looking for life to live. After marriage as newlyweds' life was going okay, I thought. Fresh off losing love and deciding I didn't want to be alone, I sent for my son and asked his mother to wed me.

To this day, I own this as my biggest mistake, for I knew not what I was doing, and this was a selfish move to avoid loneliness on my behalf. This is the moment, if any, I wish I could go back and change because I was not ready, nor did I have any life experience. I don't blame her; I blame me, for I knew what I was walking into. I didn't know what it truly meant to play that role. When you are alone and hurt, you long for what you know to be safe.

To this day, I actually do not know why except for the fact that the woman I loved supposedly got married and, well, this was my way of killing two birds with one stone. Not only would I do the same, like this was a tit for tat, but I could also have my son with me and be the man in his life. I could do what my father didn't; I could be there every day providing like my father assumed I wouldn't be able to, or so I thought.

Only problem with this scenario was once again there wasn't a blueprint, nor did I know the first thing about marriage and love and bills and being a man, so without any help, I found myself blaming at the earliest of times in our nuptials.

The first two or three years went by fast, and we were a couple, we did family things, and I tried my best to be who I needed to be for my child, but deep inside my heart, I knew for a fact I was not in love. I was happy with the situation, and that was selfish and reckless. It was like I felt I had to care for my ex-wife because of her situation in life. I won't speak on her personal setbacks here or make excuses for my actions. I cheated and went to the streets not because it was right but because I knew love had a different emotion, and I wanted so bad to find that emotion. Eventually I got my first taste while married of what love really was, and her name was Tonya Grey.

I recall meeting someone at a nightclub I would often frequent early on in my marriage, I was twenty-three or twenty-four at the time, and she was four to five years my senior. I met her at a night club called Picasso's where I was a regular at; and man, she was amazing. Tonya was accomplished and everything at the time I believed I needed to complete my puzzle. She was beautiful, corporate, old school, and in to me. That was all I needed as she was the exact opposite of the dependency my wife was at the time.

She didn't need me, and that was a turn on; it is something to say when you are wanted and not needed, and it is shown. I felt like a king when I was in her presence, or at least when I was in the bed with her. We didn't share responsibilities nor did we have any history, but we did share intimacy and an emotional bond which became the root of my life existence. The ties I created outside my home became that of which a fiend needs to scratch their itch. I longed for her and needed to be with her as much as possible. This was my first real sign that I believed I was in what love was to be.

I was willing to risk it all for this new drug, and she was not in the same stratosphere, I would soon find out.

As I said, she was my senior and had already been where I was heading in life. She had loved and lived and been through the ups and downs of a real relationship, not the play stuff I dabbled in but the real deal Holyfield of life.

She was unknowingly or possibly in full professor mode, teaching me about life, the ropes of the game, its ups and downs, and all that had to do with trying to figure out who you are in life and real love.

After several sacrifices made to find out if she was the one, she, I believe, gave in and decided to step away because of her morals after the fact and womanly intuition. I didn't tell her about my wife at first but eventually exposed myself to her. I think the lie itself plus knowing my current state and situation mentally forced her hand. I believe the fact she was a victim of a man leaving for another; she didn't want to carry that burden inside herself and expose the pain she endured on another woman's soul.

I believe she cared so much for me and knew what I was about to risk that she stepped away before I destroyed my current situation on what I now believe in her eyes was a fling with a younger guy who was lost in relations. Little did she know I was completely lost in her and in real love for the very first time and, man, how I had to create this image or find it in this way.

I begged and pleaded with her to change her mind, but I had broken her trust by forcing her to play a part in my own deceit. This was a lesson I would learn that eventually would play a pivotal role in all my future interactions. Note to self, never, ever in your life withhold information that may be life-altering from any woman as they can make their own decisions. Life-altering, now that I look back, in retrospect, that coming-to-self moment was pivotal in my future plots. It was this moment I now know that I made a harsh decision not only to be a cheat but to do it with a plan as I would cement this in my head in affirmation format.

This was not the way; this was not right, but now a cheater was born and had a blueprint to follow a script. I felt it, and I knew it was possible. I knew it was out there and accessible, and there were people who were looking for it as well. This was the worst thing that ever happened to me because I was on an all-out hunt for it, and it was intense.

I really loved being a father, I loved my wife, and I loved being a provider for what my responsibilities entailed, but I now know that, that kind of love and that new feeling of the emotion were not the same. They were on different planes. One was obligatory I felt, wrapped in a guilty bow, and the other was an emotional bond you seek to feel complete.

My now ex-wife unfortunately didn't give me that feeling at that time. Yes, I know. I was overtly disrespectful to my home, often working several jobs to support it but finding time to canvass the locals to see if love was there somewhere, anywhere, and everywhere. Was she at work, overseas, at the club, this duty station, that one?

Was she online as Black Planet, Myspace, and Together We Served started their campaigns?

The shes begun to mount, and my disrespect was in full flow. Sorry for myself, I moved in directions I now understand all failed because the entire time I searched and looked and longed, I never once took the time to ask God about my situation.

This was the time frame I began to allow myself to slip completely out of the grips of Christ and the word. This was one of if not the biggest faults within this entire issue. I chose to remove all that spiritual training I had been equipped with, and I looked to the learned behaviors that failed me while growing up.

I was a man now. I didn't have Mom and Dad to force me to go to church. I had bills and more bills along with a child and several other obstacles, and I was doing it. I felt alone, so I didn't have the time in my head to be with God or ask Jesus Christ to give me strength, help me to walk in the faith, properly keep me from ruining myself and disrespecting my last name.

I made my bed, and I was going to get out of it my way since nothing I ever did seem to get a reply prior these evolutions. I was taught you break it, you fix it; it's in your way you figure out a way around or over. There was never a moment I didn't feel that control was not in my corner. This led to a power shift and control along with pride, man's evil additives alongside ego.

I took action into my own hands to pursue a love I wish now I had just given to God. I now know that God should've been my first and ultimate love in this life since he held all my answers.

Naw, I just went off and did it my way, and I know we all know what happens when you go against God. You will be humbled over and over until you conform and hopefully before it is too late.

There is more, and yes, I have had my share of what love was to be. Later in another segment, I will attack those relationships, but these are the ones which hold a significant place in the forefront of my demise, so these are the few I will highlight. We all want to stand outside the cage and toss food at the animal trapped behind the bars. It's not until the bars are removed that we change our tone and judge not, so look at this as me removing the bars as I wish so many of us would do.

Be unapologetically you and own your drama, and if it's too much for you to swallow, well, maybe you should only take it in, in small doses, for I am who I am, and my truth is mine alone. I accept all my flaws, for I was never to be perfect but scarred into a life full of sin. Mine just may script different than yours, so cast no stone. I am at peace with myself and in rebuilding my relationship with God.

There are several instances in between these moments, but these are significant and hold extreme levels of weight. Though they are all wrong, they were mine, and before you get deep into judgment, ironically, though legally married, most of my rendezvous were while separate from my ex-wife.

Often, I would be out the home still taking care of my responsibilities, but rightfully so, she would ask me to leave, and I would. Months would go by sometimes, even years, and I would be trying my best to work, provide, survive, and all the while try and find my happy.

In the middle of these actions, my ex would always find a way to ensure I couldn't commit to whatever I was doing, and because of guilt or convenience or control, I would settle for less and not just say no.

I would oftentimes end up back at home. I think it was fear, that small part of me that knew my sons would see their father in a light that was not perfect. My guilt caused me to spoil them with material things and do things out of the norm not only because my parents couldn't and I could but because of the guilt of me not wanting to be in the house.

I asked for a divorce many times, but by now I believe she had been informed by the first wives club or the neighborhood divorce lawyers all she would acquire if she would hold out as I progressed up the ranks, so the sacrifice became sickening even to think about as I type, but what's understood in the dark comes to light in front of God, is all I will say.

After Tonya, years of playing around outside my marriage came and went, and I eventually moved to Maine. I set off for an overseas trip that would be one for the ages. So much to talk about one day. Here a Sicilian woman named Anna I fell into a deep situation with had her, I assumed, calling my wife after I left to ask her if she could have my child would be smart. There was Sherry and others all who I gave pieces of myself to in hopes someone would take me, but the Navy has a way of making sure you do not give it all, especially when you know you are to leave and move on to the next mission.

Tranise, wow, I met her while in Maine and fell for her while there. I was in the barracks alone, and it was there that we created a beautiful experience of what love could be. I ate it up until my reality was set into play and family positioned into the mix; it was then we split and went our separate life paths.

At that point, I couldn't be man enough to separate myself from my obligations I prematurely took on with my ex, and so the cycle continued, and from that moment on, I began to avoid its truth. I had seen firsthand what it did to her knowing we couldn't be an us. Fast-forward the clock many years ahead and here it is we meet again, ironically, now both stationed on the same ship. We began a small conversation which turned into a short relationship as I once again was alone. This in part turned into me completely remembering what had happened and transpired eight-plus years ago as we rekindle a situation between us.

I fell deep, and this time I was not going to allow her to escape, but it seems as if things were completely in the opposition's hands, and now this time, even though I left everything I knew, I was the one on the bad end of the stick as she told me she wouldn't be able to leave what she was doing to then give herself completely and wholly to be with me.

I spiraled out of control; I now had nothing. I was no longer in my household due to a separate issue, and I found myself homeless, drinking to mask the pain, bottles and bottles of alcohol. It was crazy how when this didn't work, I was off to my backup plans home.

I told Shae I was here and ready to be hers. I said I was willing to let the life go and that if she let me in, we could complete our picture. I originally met her in 1997 or 1998, and we had several on-and-off flings throughout the years. We were both damaged by the way of the military and always had a great relationship. One that we would lean on in times of our individual needs, and as we reunited, I was playing on emotions I believed I knew she still had. This being eleven years later and fresh off her finding me after a horrific divorce, said, "I am sorry, but I am going on a date with that guy I told you about, the Hispanic police officer we spoke on. I am going on a date with him." Angered and frustrated, I drunkenly shouted all kinds of derogatory things, and to this day, I still do not believe she knew I was really gone from my home, and honestly, I am glad she made the decision she did. How could I be upset my backup plan to a plan was not agreeing with my moves to get away from my past?

I tried to consume pills to take my own life as I sat often alone in my truck blasting The-Dream albums ironically titled *Love/Hate* and *Love vs. Money*. The songs would become the theme of my life's mistakes, and I oh so effortlessly would chant the words and cry aloud to the beats in unison as if we literally had the exact same pain.

I would blast these albums over and over crying out late into the night hours alone and most oftentimes at the beach watching the waves splash under the midnight skies. Crazy as it may sound, this would all be transpiring at the same time that I was competing to be one of the most respected individuals at my command, as the Sailor of the Year, which eventually I won, all during a homeless stint and ironically all while doing some of the most disrespectful things to myself and others over a three-year stint.

Once again proving you can be anything in the Navy, even as an impostor. You can do the most horrific things in your personal life, and as long as you don the cloth and march in step, all while singing the right tune, you can accomplish anything; you can be the super-man they show on screens.

The Navy gives you all the tools to be successful and accomplished, but what they don't give you are the tools to be a husband or wife and a good person as far as your life is concerned.

They support them and provide an exceptional outlet for them while you work and are gone often extended amounts of time, but that fine line of in and out, they say nothing about. You end up realizing your working alongside a bunch of yous and the actions are really the norm or popular.

You begin to assume the only ones who are not into the extra-curriculars are the ones at the top, and why would they be, with all the money they make? Until you realize no one is safe, it doesn't matter the rank, race, religion, gender, ethnicity, background, or knowledge level; each and every one of us has a story or knows of a story such as the ones I tell. It's so normal that if you could find someone who could say they didn't know I would be willing to give you a hundred dollars.

Long before I joined, sex and service were intertwined. This has been an issue fourscore and seven hundred years ago, I bet, but who says the soldier or sailor, the airmen or coasty is at fault? They are giving all they have to serve a country and deploy and work long hours. Who says that they are not entitled to happiness, though it may come at the most inopportune time?

Society says so, and here is where you find yourself looking down the barrel of a loaded gun, in and out of the pursuit of happiness while trying to fit into a military that shows you to advance and excel is to fit in, and to fit in is to follow suit.

Long hours, typically eighteen a day, I did, alongside some of the most beautiful individuals of the opposite sex. I was in my own form of escape. Trips abroad to some of the most beautiful places away from your norm and the drama of home creates a unique support system. When you have no concrete backing, deployments will only and typically did lead to the extra activity on an enhanced level.

Now I am not saying that all men and women in service cheat, but I will say it was both ways easily. Both men and women with much to lose so easily looked for moments of love and like the same. Deployments became great times to look for the future all while trying to see if your present was worth salvaging while gone. So many times I would return and see one who was frolicking two weeks prior at our last port call with someone, and they would be alongside me watching that person run to the arms of their final decision.

I would also see the spouse of another there with divorce papers and kids in tow ready to kick someone's ass on the ship because word was returned that they were cheating with someone else, and this was the norm.

The stories of the spouse at home who was sleeping with an ex, the neighbor, or a different service member from another ship were all too revealing. The constant what-ifs and whys, who is who in the zoo gets to a point you, end up deciding to let it all go in hopes the moments are better than missed memories, cause if you didn't, then someone else would.

Port calls would look like a matchmaker's heaven as you looked for the willing to ensure your geography was linked properly with the right travel buddies to appease the rule books.

Again, please note the military is not to blame for my poor decisions or anyone else's choices. I am not making this a telltale session or a bit to exploit anyone, so I digress. I simply wanted to lay a foundation of my learned behavior and why it was easy for me to make the decisions under the circumstances I made.

See, I was never able to really run from love, and to this day, I believe all those past memories Mom sacrificed naturally created soft holes in my being to allow pieces of emotional fear to sneak in, so as a child I cared; as a teen I cared; as a young man I cared; and as an adult, right or wrong, I cared. It looks like caring seemed to be my problem. I just could never be as hard core as most men and walk away or just say, "I quit, forget the situation, I am out," and move on.

No, no, no. LeRon always cared about something because I made each situation personal to protect my peace. It was so difficult for me to completely disassociate myself from caring, not that it was love, but it was my heart the natural emotion to care about someone. Their emotions, how they felt, what was going on, affected them, and at the end of the day, as long as both parties understood like situations, and there was no deceit and or deception, I could honestly deal with the outcomes. Because I cared, selfishly I did, and, more importantly, about my own feelings and future more than my responsibilities.

Truth be told, my normal fix was to simply find a space to sit in silence and be alone. The issue right now is having to sit in it without my normal excuse or being tied to dead matrimony or navy career which took me around the world year after year as a Band-Aid.

I am sitting in it right now alone with zero escape, nowhere to run and nowhere to hide, just me and my thoughts. I don't have my job anymore to throw me off mentally or keep me from worrying about my day-to-day actions. I don't have the lives of other sailors to put before my own in masking what pains are often felt.

I'm retired and fully divorced. The scene was set so that karma for life mistakes could force itself onto my ever being and make me see all faults from both sides and have to completely sit in it. Feel the pain, son. You are to sit and see each mistake, place after place, the destruction like the tornado you are, moving from city to city and place to place, leaving a trail of broken souls to find in fixing themselves.

While not only the change in setting was painful, but now not having control over the reason for the pain enabled anger and ways to find blame for my current misfortunes. Reading book after book, hearing song after song, and eventually looking for the next her, I ended up running out of places to run. I'm completely alone, and the silence I once found refuge in was now the most hated place to sit, so oftentimes I just cry. I now cry because I don't have the answers.

I don't have a way to place the blame on something real; there wasn't a specific moment or a specific person. I couldn't recall one memory I could say that this is where I, or it, or we, or she, went wrong. I sit in my true state only having real memories of my faults, and I am forced to simply blame myself.

Before, I could find excuse in myself, someone else, or my job. I could tell myself that I was legally married, so don't trip; you couldn't be in love anyways, or dude, you are still in between things; you always come and go; back and forth, you would never be in real love. I could say this wasn't real or wasn't love. Now I know for a fact it was me and my fear. I know my part and deserve my place but this pain.

I wonder why, if love is to be what we all seek, why in the midst of correction must it hurt to the point you don't want it? I don't think I'll ever have it now because God has made me see my ugliness to a point; I believe He sees this as all I can ever hold in one cup.

I believe He gives to us no more than we can carry, yet when you are in a mindset of hopelessness, you walk His earth in a blind state of regret, reading scripture after scripture and verse after verse often; each and every line you always cross speaks directly to a life and sin you walked.

The corners you cut, the look you had, the journey at whole so still you sit in it knowing you possibly loved and not even knew it. Yeah, now it's possibly for the final time.

Before I cry and write on, I must state this: these writings are not intended to provide anyone with self-help in life or give instructions on how to get by. I am not famous or rich with the story of how God has found mercy on me and my past transgressions to motivate you to run to the gospel. I walk my path, and these words are manicured to reach the right eyes and ears and hopes of me salvaging some years to my life.

I cry daily. I am currently without an address since my separation and in a state of despair hoping that the words simply grant me entry into the next day of life aboveground in my human and also flawed form. I write these words so I can decompartmentalize the hurt I carry. The consistent back and forth with myself and the fight I find with knowing love does exist yet loss of it is my norm. I write this to help me understand my role as I play this game of life.

I write while watching others simulate happy throughout my journey. I see people play out their fairy tales and seem to have this life thing so intact. I write knowing I have power and see how it was misused and abused, how it affected others in my past, and I sit understanding the impact in which decisions can never be replayed or replaced. I've sought forgiveness with some and understanding with others to still sit in it, knowing my role as villain and victim.

Until I put this pencil to pad, the words simply scrambled in my thoughts daily. This is where the pain resides, so no, there isn't a preface or early page of thanks; and no, there is not a script or direction, no clear tone or vibe; there isn't glory and cheer nor parties and pearls for you to notate. No gems you're supposed to store so you can use for future life challenges, no nuggets that will give you an up when your life is derailed. It's me 100 percent real life, unscripted as I think. It is the ugliness, raw and uncut, unapologetically all me.

It's my journey how I wake and decide to clear my mind. It's the years of pain I've carried and the love I know I had at one time. It's a man broken and bruised in a battle with himself able to accept all his flaws, for they are the grounds for creating something bigger and better in life.

See, I often was told, "Hey, you should read this," or, "I think his or her book will help you," when in all actuality, my artistic nature as I dove into each book took hold, and I wondered why I even opened the books in the first place. I would often end up upset as I started; I was simply depressed and angry with each author. Not because the information wasn't good or relevant; most oftentimes, just like the Bible, their words were perfectly script and in raw form. The information was what I needed.

I had never read any books or heard stories from anyone at their bottom while they were actually in it and on their back like me. I was tired of the success stories because I don't see glory in my seat. I have given and fought. I have not always been a stress case, and I actually have given and done more for others than I could equate, and here I am. I would get so upset with the stories of riches and opportunity after reading and hearing about so many fails of others it made me wonder, what about me, and why I wasn't spared before the storm. Everything I read or have read was after fact.

The Bible is the blueprint we all have to follow. It is direction, but we aren't given instruction as to its interpretation. Crazy, I believe how such a powerful manuscript is left for man to decipher its parables and passages on life and how we are to live. Why it was left for human beings to interpret and share it boggles my mind.

My intense questioning attitude and watchful eye never allowed me to properly digest the information.

I would read many other writings about how someone famous got to their rainbow, and often I would sit after a listening session and say to myself, "Self, if you had the money and fame and resources as they all do, you could tell a story of how it was oh so hard, and I did this or that to get up and at it, so I did it all, and since I did, I got blessed or had opportunity, found a partner or even love in a greater capacity."

Who writes to the ones without a vision of future? Those who already gave to this world everything they had, it seems. Who writes to those who sit alone, waiting in their dust as the time of each day passes? Who can write to the person who's loved and lost it all?

Who writes to us that understand emotional damage is not fixed with material things? Material things won't fix a broken heart. Who speaks for the twenty-six-year naval veteran who served honorably and is now 100 percent disabled and homeless?

Who talks to the man who was in love and she couldn't, wouldn't, and didn't love him in return anymore, able to simply change her locks, and move on in life and career without an explanation? I replied, "Well, LeRon, you do. You write! You sit down and tell your truth to these people, and you write to yourself, and if not one ear hears any excerpt from this memoir, at least you know that you spoke your piece.

"LeRon, you wrote your truth. You sat in it, and you reread your words for clarity and understanding and comprehension in hopes that moving forward, it would allow you some sort of peace on your remaining life journey."

So here I am unloading the boxes I carry in my person about the life I lived, and this particular box just happens to be about the reason I awake and cry daily and most often. That I miss being in love and I wish I had someone to simply wash my back.

By now, I'm sure the consensus is "Wow" and "Okay. I hear you, appreciate all the honesty, but you are one piece of work. You deserve your dirty back. You are not a man of honor," and every other negative direct analogy you can conclude. And at this very moment, I will simply say okay. You are right, and the point is for years, I have said okay, and the world was right. I agree, and then what?

How do you fix years and years of untreated trauma? I'm not a felon, a criminal; I'm not out here taking any and everything I want simply because I can. I was a lost child who became a broken kid that turned into a beaten young adult who eventually became a battered man.

Why is anyone to blame? Why can't this situation just be what happens when stories like mine are scripted how they are? Ultimately, I understand all the responsibility falls on me because I live it daily and get my place, but do you really think as I grew into this life that I sat and thought my actions were those of one who fully grasped life? Or could I have been a troubled man living life in survival mode and becoming an imposter which was always the easy way out?

If anything, be upset with the actions, be upset with my decisions but my character. Naw, I can give several examples of individuals who have made decisions way worse than mine, and the world still celebrates them as if they were saints, not sinners. You can overview the previous and GroupMe into a norm, and you'll come close, but I plan on leaving nothing to speculation. I will tell you how we got here because of one person alone, me!

It took me a very long time to see the elements which created each piece of my broken picture and accept that I may never complete my intricate puzzle, but knowing why the pieces that were in full view could be seen would be my opportunity to clean house.

I could reflect back not in therapy where most often an older Caucasian person sat across from me asking questions, as if they were the student and I was the professor, on inner city men and their ways of life, quiz tomorrow and test next week, so if you need help, just ask.

The weekly sessions blocked off for each chapter, and they would study hard wanting to know every minor detail and plot of my life. The reasoning and substance behind it all, my mindset and thinking. I was replaying over and over years of hurt and pain. We weren't working toward a fix, I felt. This led me to believe I was giving them the real-life answers to movies they watch behind closed doors they couldn't grasp. Just as I didn't understand the stock market or the meaning behind risk management and diversification at one time. I was giving them a real-life crash course of boys in the hood and menace to society. I could explain the life characters somewhat and give them a one up on their counterparts not because they cared but because they could.

So I would sit in a couple sessions and drop a few jewels off before eventually getting so tired I would quit attending. I felt that I was continually being forced to relive the same pain without any resolution insight.

Let's just say I grew so tired that I decided to push the limits. After my decided final therapy session and continued marital confusion while working on my second college degree, a bachelor's degree in general studies for promotion reasons, I, in the midst, out of the blue, took interest in taking psychology and sociology courses.

I took several classes; I took so many that before I knew it, I had completed a degree without even noticing it. I had an associates in electronics, which was basically a "gimme," do my naval background, job, and technical expertise, but the bachelors like that commercial zero to something in sixty or whatever, I dropped it all in an attempt to fix myself in that same amount of time focusing all my interests and not only learning my why but even more so, the why of each and every other person I came into contact with.

Did this kill my journey without any bullets? If so, along the route, it gave me a very honest but deadly set of skills. It gave a man without love and lots of pain the vision to seek and the tools to manipulate the pictures he allowed women to paint so fault could never be his. Right. He never asked for sex or lied about his life; he gave to those who inquired the exact answers they wanted when asked, or did I?

Maybe I was playing the lead, just like the stars in the movies, since now I would most often lead into to any ship with the normal but soon after jokingly words, "Don't mess around with me because I have a unique set of skills," and unfortunately this was very true. I had learned the art of women, not love, just women.

The psyche of why she did this and why she did that. I studied them like art learning their actions and positions on topics and subjects. What they preferred most and hated the same. Since I couldn't find love in one, I just learned them all. They became my topics of daily discussion, each uniquely built for a reason in life, but in my eyes, all not to love properly but leave men in a whirlwind of trouble while they move on and tell their friends about how he wasn't the one or how he wasn't this or that never taking ownership of their own role like I so often was forced to do.

Why did they get the good end of the stick and I was left to sit in shambles? So this was my reason. Not to be venomous, but I must say I used this set of skills to my fullest advantage even creating rules or building blocks to follow.

Yeah, I guess you can say I had my own set of personal female guidelines. They were my so-called general orders, nothing written because that would be a bit much, but yet it was etched and ingrained into my being; it was and at that time became my way of life.

See, by this time "F-love" was my song; I simply knew I could never have it, and I was to be stuck in my tumultuous situation with my son's mother whom I married not for love but out of fear, ignorance, loneliness, and pain.

Oh, and honestly, the real reason I started to write when I started along with what I previously noted is because I was on my way to Jacksonville, Florida, as my journey was ongoing, and the hurricanes were at the time pummeling the coast, so I stopped in McDonough, Georgia, to find normalcy. I ended up at a classmate's house, one I recently bumped into after thirty-plus years at my class reunion.

I decided to go to my class reunion, and the hope was to find peace and satisfaction in my current state. Maybe run into a female who was into me and have a newfound relationship start up since I was in my own head and broken. It is the behavior I knew, hurt by one, on to the next to mask the pain. The only way to get over the hurt would be to replace the name and face. While there I bumped into a bunch of people and left all my attempts at the chase in the aftermath as I believe God had me by the hand, and my steps were being placed for me.

I bumped into Sharee Smith, and she asked about my life and how things were, and we exchanged numbers, her saying, "Hit me up," and me expressing I will call and possibly stop by on my way to Florida when in all actuality, I had zero want or need to because one, well, I lost my love; two, socially, I was an impostor, and not a soul knew my current truth; three, I trust no one, so why was she so nice, and what was she looking for? Four, she, I thought, was happily married, and I didn't want to be around that fresh off my proposal failure; and lastly, if she wasn't well, my lack of feminine interaction would lead me to pursue her in my normal fashion, and I didn't want to ruin another life now that I understood my energy.

The time came, my normal routine in flow, and I sensed it was time to move on. I had worn out my welcome at my parents' home, so I was off to Florida after a month at the army base where I would set up shop to practice my new way of life. After seeing how my parents wanted their lifestyle back and my month was up, I ventured off and decided to head to Duval.

Why Duval? Well, the excuse was to fix my living situation, which meant dealing with the home I had given to my ex-wife. My house, the one thing I believed I did right while active duty. My home, which after five years of divorce, was still in my name. I took off on a mission heading to Florida and, as stated, was detoured due to the storm. I called and told her I wanted to take her up on her offer; she said come on through. So off I was on my way to Georgia.

I had a million thoughts running through my head. Remember, I was fresh off the worst moments of my life, confused, and lonely. With every bit inside of me, I told myself to act accordingly as she was very open about her current journey with Jesus Christ and God. How in the world did I let this happen? Who was scripting my way? In my head, I said, *Maybe God is giving you this opportunity to show growth or change.*

I fought my normal urges ensuring I crossed zero lines, but feeling the guilt since mentally even before traveling, I played out our dancing in the sheets and saw satisfaction, so much to the point I expressed my concerns to her.

She understood and stated she was in the same boat as it is natural and normal to want to be loved and experience all it has to offer. Me fresh off my breakup and her newly divorced, we were in the same boat moving in opposite directions, I believed. In the end, I was happy she understood my ordeal, calling my attention toward scriptures that provided some needed insight, and she topped it off with a visit to her church before my travels.

I took off to Florida on a separate expedition, I believe I passed Florida's test of old faces and the temptation to fall back into some of the traps I previously fell for. It is very ironic that after years away from Jacksonville, I decide to go to a cigar bar, and who is there in the midst? Felicia. Yes, I see one who played a pivotal role in the chapter which was Duval. She walked in and watched me from a distance ensuring I was who I looked like, and then she approached. It was awkward, the conversation, because it was the test I believe I needed to ensure I passed.

Soon after another person who was intricate in my way of life arrived, and it was like days of old, me in a room full of chance, yet this time I was terrified to be the person I once was. I felt like I was being watched by God, so each movement was orchestrated as to not let Him down.

Vanessa was one who spent several months going through a homeless stint while being separated from service in Virginia with myself, and our associate Shawn allowed us to stay with him. She knew of my arrival in Florida, and I so wanted to thank her for the support over the years. The issue is when you are in your storm and life is altered, others may be tested as well, and they only know or see you as one person.

Old emotions, I believe, erupted as maybe I was believed to be who I was still. She cast her net, and I avoided being caught because the only thing I knew was my actions needed to show growth and not stagnation. I took off a couple weeks later without notifying either of my departure as the nights got longer, and the days seemed like torture while ridding myself of the stench from my past. In it all, I felt accomplished because I was able to sit with each and have a genuine conversation about the past, and I apologized for any and everything I may have done to each. This, though late in my eyes, still was progress as they both issued me understanding and recognition of their roles in the situations as well.

Florida wasn't my typical visit, yet it was very much so necessary, I now believe. I went back to another place where I had set my trail ablaze and was able to see a couple things in retrospect. I saw people I surrounded myself around still doing the same things, in the exact same places I was in while there. This was a sign that growth was not relevant in most. I also saw several individuals who were a part of my way of life and how they were impacted by me, and it showed in decisions they made in men and how they were going about their choices, because I left somewhat of a mark on their beings. This saddened me because it wasn't fair to leave a mark so deep on a person that they looked to find a duplicate in the person you were. It is not fair to them or the people they were dating.

I returned to Sharee's house with more spiritual questions and a wanting to attend her church again while I was still wrestling with my personal needs. One night before I was to leave, she came in, and we spoke, and she eventually said, "LeRon, you ought to write about all the anger and pain you carry."

She said, "God is telling me that in order for you to begin to heal and move forward to the glory he has for you, you need to cleanse yourself of the pain and anger you carry, and he says you need to write."

That said, I stated, "Okay, I will. I promise I'll start tomorrow," and when night shifted unto daylight, I sat, I cried, I stared, I cried, I got angrier, I cried harder, and then I paused, got a pad and a pencil out, and started to write.

*****

Waking up alone once again, the weather is back and forth, off and on. It's hot then cold, a sure sign that things in the world as I knew were shifting. For years the norm was apparent in season. Growing up the seasons were very much observed by the temperature and definitive shifts in nature. I now feel this ugly shift as summer temps intermingle and mix with wintery, frigid nights all in the same day let alone in the same hours. Often, I look confused as I wear the same clothes day in and day out.

Covered in my Navy hoodie and pajama pants with slides barely myself and inching out the bed every morning upset that I even have to arise to follow the same plan over as it was written the day before and the day before and ironically the day before that. There's no need to wear the designer items or get dressed to the nines when I feel less than zero.

My life is at a standstill; there isn't any change, just the monotony of repetition. I feel dirty. I don't care about bathing. Who is around anyways except Ratchet? My ultimate excuse was its fine since my hot water doesn't work. I wash at the gym when I get the strength to attend. I simply feel like I look, and they are both in unison. The ugliness I carried inside is now not only just emotionally disturbing because it is consistently felt. I now also look the part.

I look just like the people I drove by on corners giving handouts to. This doesn't sit well with me since I still can't put the pieces to this location in my Google Maps and see how I ended up at this humiliating destination.

Pastors preach about the bottom, the dark, and how many righteous individuals looking for something are here, placed by God to sit in hopes they can eventually find themselves. Find themselves deep down inside themselves in it, with nothing to reach for but faith. No material possession to lean on, no family or friends, no loved ones to guide them, and no information to assist your search.

The dark places God puts man in to humble them. The dark places that break spirits and kills egos when you are removed from the crutches of your immediate life. The Band-Aids placed on your existence in hopes to find healing are removed so the ugly scars are exposed in your pain. All for a purpose because the light must be appreciated. The dark is a place to be molded, I believe, so that the light is understood. When and if your allowed to see again, you will now appreciate to a point you ensure your return to the darkness is never an option.

The brighter day but darkness of my soul would never properly align is my feelings. No matter what or how I try, the harsh reality feels like I've been unfortunately sentenced to life in my own head. I've been spiritually, physically, mentally, and financially sentenced to a full bid where the days go by one by one, and the pictures are there all in high definition on repeat unseen, feeling blinded by the past and my humanly needs.

This is the very reason that I stay up late at night and arise as the next day is already in process really hoping to minimize reality. The fact that nightly I go to sleep with my own pain as a constant reminder of what love was in the form of a dog. April 22, 2020, months before she would begin the turmoil which was my new life, a dog was bought as a birthday gift at eight-plus weeks old. This Yorkshire terrier who I fell in complete love with, wondering why she up and bought me a $1,500 child before deciding to bail, still confuses me.

I say to myself, it is the sign of man leaving a mother with a child. I attempted to be the father to a child she so wanted. I went beyond my own wants to assist her with the blessing of a child not once but twice as both IVF attempts failed with zero refund after the efforts. Nothing but time invested and resources drained as the future did not involve our own.

I now see to some degree in a different light what it's like. I've been given this puppy to care for as she went off into life to excel and do all she wanted. Me left to struggle and interact daily with a memory of what we were. Daily growing angrier and more upset at the situation but in the same breath not being able to just rid myself of the pup I would say she did it to keep me out of the streets while she left me for two years forward deployed to Rota, Spain, to serve this country.

The typical Navy relationship I guess it is. I rise and see him, never fully knowing the truth as to why she did it if her vision was a selfish one in the end. My life would actually be a lot easier to maneuver without the emotional attachment of this puppy, feeding him, walking him, cleaning up daily after him, attention given, and every other aspect of what it is to support one who can't support themselves.

Was this karma for what my ex-wife went through? Was this payback for what may have been her life if things went through as expected? Who knows. I can only believe he was here for whatever is meant, so I do my duty as prescribed and feel lost while acting as if I am okay.

See, for love to have been the motive, you would assume this manuscript wouldn't even be necessary. Three-story home, five vehicles, all the latest clothes to our liking, and travels monthly. As I stare at this forced responsibility every day, I realize he's actually a huge piece of why moving on is not simple.

You arise, give thanks half-heartedly, let him out, and sit in an awkward silence picturing your past life and all it was. The tears form, regret lines up, anger amasses, and the pain ensures you deal and then challenges you to face off.

Truly aware of why weaker minds turn to habits or go insane since it's a warfare most are not capable of being in. This is confusing is an understatement. Now my entire life seems to have been a blueprint on how you have to deal, so why was this my end point? I think aloud, "I don't wanna die like this." I don't ask any more about how to win in life, how to succeed, or how to achieve the American dream but how to arrive each day able to deal.

Somewhat numb in life, I think of my current location and the irony that from where I currently sit, there are two directions of travel which would take me to two lives that truly helped create me as I am. From McDonough, Georgia, ironically, I sit in between LaGrange, home of the woman who first grabbed my heart and emotions but would also be the first to crush my frame just as fast.

LaGrange, Georgia, is where Sophia was from. I met Sophie in 1993, and she was to be, in my eye, my future. I had never been anywhere in life. As for love and now the Navy provided free room and board on an all-out twenty-six-year ride which went around so many different parts of the world allowing me to meet amazing individuals. Some regrets, yet I had the knack to never create any tension. Hence those learned rules of my creative life I'll speak on later.

The other direction of travel would lead me to Stockbridge, Georgia, and another woman who eventually would not only play an important role in my extracurricular but who would become an angel I would hurt.

I met her fifteen years after the above meet, and the emotions of my selfish needs were by this time worn on my sleeve as I was a seasoned womanizer by this time. There was no fear in explaining my life and how professionally I had great future, but personally I was a shell of who I could be. I was able to express every piece of my heart to one who would simply listen and harbor my pain with me as she oftentimes did.

Eventually those conversations became the gateway to empathy and soon a full-fledged relationship while living with her full-time. I was homeless while having a home, and she took me in at a time when two others pushed me to the side as I spoke on. She saw the daily struggle to show up and perform my duties and offered me assistance and refuge which I would take full advantage of. The problem was I had my crutches and a fear of being forced to commit to permanently being with her and prematurely being a part of what I believe her future saw.

She came or was placed in my world at a time I was truly trying to figure the Navy and advancement out along with my personal being. Severely broken I was at my then lowest as another heartache was fresh and the wounds were evident, and she knew it. We worked together, and I found safety in our open life conversations. I exposed my weaknesses in life. My spirit was revealed in truth as to my extra-curricular in life and my ignorance in decision-making. I can honestly say it was her who retaught me that emotional security was real no matter the gender. Bigger than that, she was one who would go on to stand so close to me and for me that my own rules I used to justify my lifestyle would be the same rules to disrupt our lives. If it was one, I regret leading into my destructive ways she would be the one. She would be the one I wish I could remove my stink from as she was an extremely pure soul subject to my foolery.

Our story was real, and it spanned years. Now that I look back on it, the obvious pain one feels I can only assume is if they see you as their end goal and you act as one with someone else. Elsewhere after the fact you are now in the relationship, they saw for themselves. I now understand I can't lie as I knew what she wanted, and knowing this still hurts to this day. I know I only did to her what the latter did to me eighteen years prior, which still is no excuse for my actions because I knew what it was going to feel like to be her, so to speak.

The pain that I feel currently is more likely the same pain she felt once I completely moved on. When you are on the outside looking in, you never understand what someone goes through, especially if they don't inform you the intricacies of the emotions they hold. Most people don't talk openly about how they really feel, which leaves the other person to assume that they are okay when really, they aren't.

Most people go on in life with these ugly situations attached. They have established soul ties, created without expectation. Both sides create outcomes and excuses. You both hold grudges; mine were just for ignorant reasons as I believe she had every right to display anger in any fashion she so chose. This creates toxicity in a spiritual world and goes unanswered for, until eventually God steps in and takes a hold of both parties to create mutual agreement amongst the stars.

A price has to be paid, and how it is paid, well, who knows, but please believe when wrong is done in the dark and it is brought to the light, there is a price that is paid. Most times often it is throughout pain and hurt before finding some sort of light at the end of a tunnel. By that point, both parties are no longer entertaining each other, so you move forward hoping to not create the same mistakes again in a future relationship.

Stockbridge, Georgia, is where Nikki was from. I met her in 2008 while stationed on the USS *Harry S. Truman*. I can say she was a good person, a real friend who I would let too close to me. Nikki carried every single trait a broken man needs to be able to simply move day to day in life, and she became my crutch, and I can honestly say I became hers as she saw me as her future.

The real killer was knowing that she was forced to socially and, from a distance after years of supporting every aspect of my being, watch me fall in love with another woman. She watched my online antics as I gave all my love out loud to a newly found person after finally severing ties with my wife in a legal manner. After years and years of torturing each other, my now ex-wife and I separated, and immediately I went into the arms of another. I was in tune with Lakeisha and wanted it to be my forever as this was the exact thing she was never privy to for years and years being left in the shadows and outside my social circles.

I love and was finally able to freely fall for someone since I left my wife, and I now understand that Nikki truly had real reason to be mad since the man she picked up and dusted off chose to find peace and serenity in another woman. I can only imagine what it would feel like to invest and sacrifice all of your time, emotion, and self to someone regardless the situation to see them eventually grow to be someone you knew they were before they knew and then see them gallop off into the sunset with someone else, doing all the things you envisioned the two of you not only doing but being happy doing it.

Oh, wow! How ironic as now, I mean right now, as that person, I honestly get it. I can only imagine the nights of tears and struggle to gather yourself because now it is I that is paying that price. I could never fault her for being completely destroyed by my current situation, yet if she only knew, finally finding peace and understanding that I now pay for my mistakes.

I sit broken, torn, battered, and bruised just as she possibly had prior to this entire situation happening. I never created any false dreams or painted picket fences or placed pictures with puppies in our forever happy in her purview. My mistake was I did everything in action as if it was to be. This was evident, I'm sure, in her eyes. I think my actions then were so easy because of my obligations, though separated, I led her to believe that one day it was achievable and possible.

The actions above come from my poor learned behavior. Back in 1993, I was just a newly minted sailor, fresh out of A school, forced to transition after making and establishing so many great relationships. I wasn't ready for new just this fast. I didn't want to leave or change life; I was just getting used to this new freedom in Memphis. I had met a crutch I now know, and her name was Sophia. She and I were inseparable, and after months of daily interaction, I saw her as my forever. No physical activity between us at that time, so it had to be real as this was the way I understood it from the Bible.

After I left, I heard Sophia and another man, a marine supposedly married; he was then my competition; he was the guy who took my girlfriend years ago when I was in high school. I apparently had never repaired myself from that psychologically, and it hurt all over again as I heard the laughs and felt the same pain years later as I once did, so in turn I shut down.

I suffered my first real-life breakdown over a woman I loved. I had given her my intent of a forever, my heart. I believe this was a huge turning point in my learned behavior. The Navy had sent me to San Diego, California. As a young man, nineteen years old to be exact, and heck, I had never been out the hood unless it was to go to my grandparents' house.

Now all within a year, I spent eight weeks in Chicago, ten months in Memphis, and now I am in San Diego, California. Talk about a real culture shock and social conflict all wrapped in one. I see why my emotions were everywhere. I didn't have anything stable, I believed, since I had zero relationship with God. This would be the beginning of me learning how to start, stop, cut off, and move on. I would get used to cutting off, alone, start over, and repeat. Yes, I say this: the Navy really does, had, and has taught me how to be a machine. It's just unfortunate that our military creates some of the greatest misfortunes its employees must face. This becomes learned behavior where you show up, you show out, and you move on.

In your personal life, you arrive, you cut off, and you start over. You move on, you arrive, you cut off, you start over, you move on, and you do this over and over and over again, and in my case, in a twenty-six-year military career, it became an art knowing the fact I could show up to a completely new city, state, or country; meet as many people; and create as many relationships as necessary to survive, and just as fast as they were created, they would be removed as you move on. Comfort after Sophia, I learned it was never an option.

When it was all said and done, I would be moving on to the next place not knowing that this behavior will become my biggest downfall creating adversity and leaving soul ties so many places that it was inevitable for them to eventually interlink and become this mass that was so big and so heavy to carry that it would create the force that would eventually be one of my greatest regrets in life.

My biggest issue, as far as Sophia was concerned, was how could she get engaged, the things we talked about, the life we planned at nineteen? Young, educated, both graduating aviation electronics technician school, the time invested day in and day out, my sacrifice and personal time traveling with her to console her pain when a family member died, meeting her family—these were all the things that shown me future, so how could she feel obligated to accept another man's presentation of love just that fast? What about me?

I later found out that it was all a lie. The story of her wedding was a lie told to me by someone we both considered to be a friend. The story was told to me by one who knew we were an item, and she was in a bad relationship herself. She was in a marriage which was under attack, and I was in the middle of it all. We spent off time together in between her problems, and I became as much of a personal distraction to her as her real issues were in her household.

I slept with her without knowing what was under her intent. I saw it as a way to feed my own ills in life. A grown woman who saw this kid as a means of satisfaction personally, why not take the ride was my ignorant way of thinking. I can recall the time spent sleeping with her, and to think she was pregnant carrying the child of a womanizer, so I was told. I felt low, but ignorantly, I also felt accomplished as the feeling was one I longed to have; it was a form of love that I learned from years prior.

She was showing me all I felt I needed to survive at that moment, and the stories would never be told. I believe the majority of my days I blamed Sophia for ruining my life and how I approached mine. Now I know I created what I sit in, and it started as I made excuse after excuse for the why. I acted and never expected the actions to have penalty, and for years, they always had a way of paying me back.

I think because I was nineteen with issues unresolved like being a young father, promiscuity, the fact I barely graduated high school, being the worst drug dealer in all Missouri, and losing a baseball scholarship all played a part, but it was my decision-making that was the problem.

When I met Sophia, I placed my heart and my future on the gambling table and lost it all, I assumed. I blamed her for years for me getting married. After learning the truth, I only shifted blame and blamed Tommi for the lie about Sophia's nuptials, which played a role in me asking my ex to wed, feeling she forced my hands.

Really, I know now I am and was always the only one who needed to be blamed, for if I had not fell for devilish actions and walked away, I would still have had my chance. My weakness was now exposed. I have now, for a second time in as little as four months, found that women were my weakness. While in Memphis, I had an interaction with a woman I met at the club which ended horrifically, and now this and they both were exposing me to the ugliness of life and sex in ways I was not prepared to deal.

I wonder if I was to resist temptation, maybe Tommi wouldn't have had a problem seeing her two friends wed, vice creating hate and discontent between us, pushing us both further away from each other.

Through it all, I finally had an opportunity to be somebody. I felt alive, even after the self-proclaimed black sheep of the family who couldn't seem to get anything right assumed he had zero options there actually was a fresh start. The navy was my way out, and even though I had so much trouble conforming to military service and being told what to do by white men just as I had prior to joining, it was evident that I eventually had to conform and make this work.

I didn't see any other options, so as much as I told myself the navy would not be my forever, deep down inside my heart, I think and know to this day my soul knew that this was it. This was it, and it was for the long haul. From day one, this was my option and my way of getting a second chance or third or fourth or fifth or sixth in my case.

I left Saint Louis with nothing but the hope that maybe just maybe a slow kid, challenged, so to speak, from Jennings, Missouri, who couldn't do much could work hard to learn a life skill and provide for his child. After Chicago, eight weeks of boot camp, I was off as stated above to Memphis or Millington, Tennessee.

Never had I been away alone as a man single to mingle, and I was all in, and the beauty was no social media, no cell phones. At most you had access, if you were lucky, to a beeper or pager, as we used to call them. This meant that my everyday life was just that—it was truly my real everyday life.

The Sophia situation played a huge part into my marriage choice which was eventually to my son's mother, but really it was a bundle of lies and deceit which led me to wed. I know for a fact my previous reckless behavior was what led me to wed. I believe God knew that sickness I allowed into my being as a child after years of blame was still there and dormant. He knew my sexual exploits were ready to act, and I was weak in spirit, let alone unable to reason and say no to a woman willing to give herself to me in acts of love. Now that I was able to come and go and make my own decisions, my sexcapades were ready to be played out in real life. So to slow me down before I continued to rage, I was placed in a time-out to see if I would change directions.

I wasn't in love with Leigh; I loved her as my son's mother and one I grew up with. I didn't hate her, but how did I know she was to be my wife or the woman of my dreams?

I had never lived or done anything other than be a kid in the hood with her alongside for the ride. We created a son who I love with all my heart, but in love, I know for a fact I was far from it, but I also knew I had a dependency with being with someone, and she filled that void growing up.

She was what I knew. She was my comfort zone and sense of normal. I only felt real, true adult on your own love once at this time, and it was Sophia. How ironic, the one I hadn't slept with. Instead of understanding it was something tangible, accessible again, and able to be found and had properly, I went into a vicious shift that would not only change me and who I was but so many lives after me as well along the way.

The more I write, the more I see I have been my own worst enemy. I have created so much damage and destruction that I can only thank God for allowing me to suffer in silence as most would not even have the ability to have a voice this late in their demise. I question, why me, and wonder why the dirt done to me was allowed to play out as I grew into a person without restraint when given opportunity to be with women. I always found my past as a reason to blame for my actions vice asking for understanding and help to overcome the issues in my life. I was touched, and it was not right, so why am I forced to deal with this ugliness? End of the day, my untreated acts led to a life of ignorant choices I would have to own for years to come as each and every encounter became a gateway into my own earthly hell.

My List of Ignorant Rules

Ignorance is bliss, they say.

Rude, impolite, ill-mannered, bad-mannered, unmannerly, ungracious, discourteous, insensitive, uncivil, ill-humored, surly, sullen, boorish, oafish, loutish, crude, coarse, vulgar, gross—these are all words which describe what you are about to read. As a man, you will see how insensitive I became after years of hurt and untreated pain. I became so calculated I assumed I was not able to give or properly receive love, so I was willing to sit in my sin. I was now trained. Military structure worked for the day-to-day business, so why wouldn't rules work for my personal life? The issue is the man who created this trash was broken, and so his rule was broken.

Rules were put in place to help us resolve issues and overcome obstacles. Rules give us structure and guidelines. If the rules were followed, you had a way forward, you had a way around, and in case there was an issue, you had a rule that moved you along without much damage being sustained.

Rules for this and rules for that. Rules you are taught to abide by. Each rule was to be followed to a tee, in all aspects of life, so naturally I assumed that a set of rules would help ease the ignorance I was to create and endure.

Crazy thing, some rules are simply ignorant, and because we give them a title or name, it doesn't mean they are just, but that maybe they are just ignorant or any of the words associated from above.

Rule #1: Always allow the woman to make her own choice and/or decision. This was something I came up with after learned behavior, studying, watching women when it's not about the physical and you make it about the circumstance you learn that if they make their own decisions regardless the outcome, they cannot hold you ultimately accountable.

You never have to lose sleep at night. This was my number one way out and how I was able to compartmentalize different faces and moments without having any stress tied to the situation.

As long as I was unhappily in mine knowing my ex-wife has zero intent on correcting herself to appease our family, I found justice knowing that whoever the individual was on the other side of my situation ship, as long as they understood the choices being made were both agreed upon, I felt zero guilt moving forward, and if things didn't work out for whatever reason or I moved on or they moved on, it was easy because choices were made to play whatever role or part in the situation at hand.

Rule #2: Remember you are legally married, LeRon, and you give them your current state and real place within your marriage. This one was simple. I used to go out in the late '90s and take the ring off, and I became that man in the nightclub without his wedding ring on or with it in his pocket or in a car or in a bag too oftentimes after drinking or some other situations occur you forget and you have to explain once you enter your home.

I then saw several men who simply wore their rings, and it seemed as nothing was different; they still live the same lifestyles, and many women, for whatever reason, were choosing these guys. I associated it with the ability for someone to make a choice, so I in turn always wore my ring after the fact and told my truth leading off most often with, "I'm married," and I found that most women really didn't care.

I think they saw your situation as yours and theirs as a moment, so it was easy to engage, and when you are not looking at someone as a physical asset regardless of how you meet, especially in my view where I think or thought everyone brought a commodity or something to the table, it was easy to miscue. Eventually most of these relationships spun into physical which had nothing to do with the initial reasoning behind our meet, yet lo and behold, I purposely did a lot of the meetings knowing the longer someone was around me, the opportunity truly would exist for a physical interaction eventually. If it did, okay. If it didn't, okay, but the fact that I had placed myself in a position to be readily accessible was my own fault.

Rule #3: Always cater and be compassionate. This had nothing to do with wooing or trying to get someone to come from outside of their comfort zone; this was just to note that in the society I lived in, all black men were not created equal, let alone man. Women begin to advance in life alone and no longer need us as a counterpart because they were given access most oftentimes more than us to do it themselves.

I found that being a gentleman, opening doors, pulling out chairs, buying gifts, the simple things in life took you further with them personally. I didn't have to come out of character and not be myself. I didn't have to be a person in a song or video or like her favorite artist, actor, entertainer, her ex, her future; all I had to be was me.

These simple things were not being done by the majority of men in the world no matter where I went, so I acted the same, and it was received with open arms over and over again which simply solidified the fact that you didn't have to be anyone other than yourself. I genuinely cared and had a free spirit open to entertain someone that wasn't perfect just as myself, and those flaws eventually created lines which allowed like souls to have conversations that go into the wee hours of the night.

Those conversations created lines that eventually created a basis of trust which when the darkest moments of your darkest moments come to fruition, all you have is each other to lean on, and it's those moments I made my biggest mistakes. It's those moments, decisions on my part were made which were not bound under what God sees us to be as His children. I made decisions for my own selfish reasons in life; I made decisions which I thought were fruitful for my moments.

Rule #4: Always be soft and vulnerable. I knew there were enough hard souls out and about, so I set that standard. This tied into the above most oftentimes. Women that I met, had the opportunity to meet, speak with, or be around, would be infatuated with the guy who was in the streets. The guys who had the force behind them to make a room feel fearful. The dude who commanded attention and could enter a room and everyone would look in awe.

I myself didn't have the resources personally to hold that title, yet eventually I found a way to create my own abilities in those same rooms. I never completed the full missions of goon-ology and being a street guy, but I got close enough. I had enough stories or tales of my real-life escapes from death, dealings with drugs, sexual escapades, and the likes coming from Saint Louis that when conversed about, they created a parallel because how could I have these stories and yet be so kind, caring, and soft? Overemotional as a male, I would always relate it back to my mother as I stated earlier in this writing, I cared. I believe she placed something in those cracks in my cold heart which never allowed me to be a killer, and thank God, or else I'd be in prison.

Those nights where I could sit and have a sensitive side with someone created an escape from my ugly reality I often complained or fought openly and often about. When I couldn't confide in my closest relatives, I did with them. I couldn't talk with my ex-wife; we often fought, and typically during our fights, she would use what I told her in confidence against me, and nothing felt worse than hearing words spoke out of pain being used against you.

Rule #5: If they give themselves to you, you do your best to make them feel different. Whatever that meant in word, I would try my best to execute. At this moment, everything else was already in play; there was nothing left said or needed to be said. I knew who I was to this person, and I knew who they were to me. Basically, life roles were established, and this moment was when decisions were made by both parties, and by this point, both parties left with a satisfaction that was worth every bit of the weight.

I always wondered why I couldn't find this moment within my household, but I asked myself often in a previous life, did I try? I can say yes. My entire relationship with my ex-wife was not full of cheating. There were moments of respect. There was an attempt several times that I tried; I just believe I never had true intent on making this my forever. No matter how I tried or how much she forced it, I always knew I was never in original love and that there was something else out there.

I knew I did not want to be like my parents, forced to be in a situation because of the situation not because of it being one that was supposed to be real. So in turn I tried my best to do my best when it came to my extra. If they gave of themselves without the typical relationship hassles of arguments, fights, drama, being extra, and were always forward and up-front with their expectations of me, I would go the extra mile to make them feel better than before or different from their normal even if it was just for those moments spent. I did it.

Rule #6: Take the time to learn them and everything about them that you can, finding out what actually makes her tick. This became an obsession. I would spend days upon days and hours upon hours conversating, questioning, looking, inquiring, and the sort to know every single thing about a person who was uniquely put together on this earth to be a specific way.

I believe that at that time it was just for personal gain or control. It was some sort of sick warfare, a strategic tactic, because the more I knew about how she worked, thought, and acted, I could avoid future conflict.

I could control all the situations I had zero control over especially since this was all unchartered water we would both be wading in. I even believed I could control the physical because even though most oftentimes physical was involved, it wasn't my motivating factor by this point. I actually fell in love with people and the interactions; the physical was my way of creating a bond.

I believed and hoped to secure something. What that something is I will never ever know, but there was always a something. Maybe it was buying time until my next travel to the next duty station or the next person or the next situation; maybe I was hoping that this person would be the right person or the person to get me out of my marriage, who knows. I always ended up creating a relationship that would follow me, a soul tie that would carry me to my next situation, something that I knew I could always fall back on because I learned so much about so many people.

Rule #7: Don't sleep with anyone just because. Do not be reckless; this is real life. Still that ties into everything prior do my situation. I justified my actions by not being physical or having a physical only intent. I was never a one-night-stand type of guy, believe it or not. It was hard to meet and sleep with someone. I've always wanted to get in to someone's being and create some sort of emotional attachment so that the physical felt a specific way.

I never believed in physical interaction without some sort of emotional tie until now as I sit without a physical attachment. Lacking in the subject, so to speak. I believe relationships, situation-ships, friendships, all ships where two individuals have specific needs, and those needs eventually on both ends are expected to be met will be. Some people find that need met early on and possibly upon first meet; others take time so that they have a better understanding as to what they are venturing into.

I believe those situations allow for me to be placed where I am mentally and physically now. Sitting in a need for some sort of interaction to the point that it drives me crazy. I long for it, I lust for it, I look for it, and even if I find it, I am now fearful of making a move because of my past transgressions, so I have a certain level of respect for it now. Love, that is.

A level of respect I didn't have for the love that I had when I had it, and now that I've lost that love due to a lack of respect, I have a fear of moving forward with anyone because I know who I was. I apologize for my ignorant ways, God. Please spare me as I have sat in enough silence and understand moving forward what is expected of me and my actions to be a humbled and productive soul. For my sins, I repent, and more so, I ask for forgiveness when you see it fit. Amen.

Life's Actions Destined for Failure

Like I stated, I was never taught how to love, so eventually through pain, hurt, heartache, and suffering all while walking in my truth, I forced my soul into a revolving door of ups and downs with numerous women.

An inner-city kid from Saint Louis, I would have never ever thought I would have met females from around the world who would play such a major role in my ignorant way of thinking about life as a man. Yet here I sit thinking, wow, LeRon, you did a lot of stuff. I did a whole lot of things; some I now regret, and some I wish I could have had the opportunity to do the right way as I look back in time. To think I actually, as things evolved, took the time to create a so-called self-protection plan, a backup kit for every single situation I would eventually encounter except for the very situation that would downsize my entire way of life and leave me confused after all the years of strategizing as to what my space in this life was to be.

I had full on protection from all but myself. Full protection from many horrors in life but not from love because love or lack of it properly is what created that ignorant list, I followed. That ignorant list of rules to avoid life circumstances. That ignorant list, oh, such an ignorant list of things, thoughts, regards, and disregards for what was real in life.

I believe you cannot beg, plead, barter, or bargain against God's will. This means you cannot rewrite His expectations of us as His children, let alone create ways to circumvent His commandments. Love in its purest form is a natural emotion that cannot be contemplated or plotted against. You can never assume one person involved in love will not lead from true emotions. This is that dark hole where my soul is left to think about everything that I previously had put in place as barriers to protect against the current pain.

The wrecking ball of an ideology that would not only plague many others along my life's journey, but it would eventually smack me so hard I would find myself naked in a closet with Trey Songz on repeat, right before my heart was shattered and pieced together to obliterate once again by the same woman, Lakeisha.

I wonder why me so many days, as I recollect the faults of my life. I guess I had it coming, some could say. I rebut that it takes two, and I never forced myself into anyone's life, any woman's bed, let alone their hearts.

Life was bound to catch me slipping, but in reality, I didn't think I would really ever find love or love find me. I figured this was another chapter in a story I'm being forced to tell. I had all the other pages in my horrific story lived out, but it wasn't finished; it needed that dramatic ending, and here she came in full force. On cue, Lakeisha hit me with words open-ended without closure with the force of a Mike Tyson jab from his heydays after the bell first rung. After all I just wrote, about old love and my life's flames, the pencil scripts back to one, and I'm saddened and teary-eyed hoping to not cry.

My back is unwashed another night. Though I scrubbed all I could, contorting in a friend's shower currently shared by four with zero assist, I still hurt, and I'm intimately confused. I dry myself off looking at a troubled man in the mirror left to wonder if this is my new life sentence, my new normal. Wake, cry, sad, gym, ratchet, sleep, regret, sad, replay, and repeat.

I wonder if Lakeisha thinks of me; I wonder as I cry if I ever mattered to her. It is so hard to live I feel as I can't just let it go. I broke every rule for this moment, and there wasn't a plan, so now what? What do you do when you played a foul game, thinking you could create your own rules and just walk away when you felt like walking away without paying for the damage you did prior?

When you were playing the fool, it was fun because your actions didn't hold true consequence. Now someone has beaten you at your script, and as the ring leader in your own circus, you find it hard to believe the last laugh is not with you but on you. You say you weren't ready, you didn't expect the plot twist or turn, and maybe in this life real love isn't to be. Maybe, just maybe, the prison you currently serve time in, in your mind, is to run concurrent, and wow, if so, I don't know how long I can survive, but it would never be enough to replace the ignorance I previously took part in.

Tears currently racing down my face, I try and see through the pain to continue on. I wonder if God sees me crying, if He knew and knows my real heart and the truth behind my situation. I wonder if God knows the past damage I was victim to and gets the reasoning for why I committed such atrocities. If He saw all that I did and done, where it came from, and how it truly was something I didn't create on my own, I know I wasn't born like this.

Would God take into factor all the moving parts? Everything that comprises the ugliness, the lifelong search for real love in a pure form, the mistakes, the things that happened to me before I could even understand what living life was. Does God really get the numerous choices made and why I decided to take the routes I did? Can he retrace my situations, circumstances, my pains, the reason I cried as a child, and still cry as an adult?

I yelled out, "Why me?" from years of hurt, "Why me, God?" "Why?" If I gave myself to you after years of being forced to attend service day in and day out, vacation Bible studies, deacon and trustee junior boards, boys choir, play after play, speech after speech, "Why me?" I ignorantly felt that not once in life was I ever given an explanation or a reason. Not once was I offered anything but more pain for the right I did and even more pain for every wrong.

Growing up with this way of thought led to blame. My ignorance in blaming God for not liking me as if He didn't have more to do with His time aside of pick on me. My foolish ways led me to believe I was ostracized on purpose and a throwaway, so why not just live how the world expects you to? You will never be more than the worst, so if you achieve that, then you are what the world expects.

To blame the supernatural or spirit world is easy since you either believe or you do not, and like love since I believed in God, I felt I truly must be cursed, the black sheep as assumed. I must be so bad of a person in a good person's body that this is the line left for me to walk. I believe He knows all; He knows I won't physically harm anyone or myself in my emotional mind state, so I am tested and pushed to my emotional limits over and over to see if I have come to a better version as to why I am shown favor with each day I am above ground. I believe His gift to me is to still be above ground, and as I humbly sit, He awaits me to repent and understand my real place on this earth.

I sit in it all, crying day in and day out. Left in life not by choice but simply because of how He wrapped me as a being. I believe in fairy tales, the remixes to songs, and happy endings. He knows I believe in possibilities and chance.

He knows my life is the perfect picture of multiple rolling hills where you go up to transit down and follow suit because life is hard. I come to expect my scenario, darkness daily without light, so He also now sees up close my lack and confusion when I have zero control. The pain that covers my being is now consuming my cloak, without answers to questions and never ever being told or shown properly why He is punishing my soul from the inside out.

Maybe I deserve it. Naturally I ask again, "Lord, what about me?"

I'm sure all I just script is from pain, for God sees all and knows all yet didn't stain me or so-called blackball my existence, at least I hope not. After all I've seen, done, and/or been a part of, I have to wonder at times. In life what we believe are test, setbacks, failures, and obstacles actually somehow or some way maybe just maybe they are divine detours for correction.

I have continued recently to hear and learn about steps and how God has created each of us for a path to a purpose, yet I struggle with why my walk has been so hard. I am then told it's life, and you make your own earthly decisions. If so, then why have all mine felt as if they were wrong or not of godly choosing? I take it that part in the Bible I've not crossed. The pastors and other spiritual leaders I listen to are not in tune, or is it simply me questioning my faith again?

I would say the latter is the answer to my issue. I will never get to play out the songs and videos made for love. I will never find my happy or get to accomplish what life really has. I have only myself to blame. Normally I am okay with my faults, yet there is something about this time that doesn't allow me to believe the future has light ahead. All I envision in my future are more lonely days, more tears, and still that dirt left center of my back.

Before I move on deeper into my personal thoughts, writing about my life, I want you, whoever you are, to know I am only scratching the surface of a lifetime of loveless nights. My life is a movie in itself the most acclaimed author couldn't fabricate. It may sound like something you would read in some of the most intriguing novels scripted by the most competent hands, but actually the story of my time on earth is that of a simple man in some of the most compelling situations one could find themselves in.

I feel like there was a tug of war with my soul. For everything God was doing for me, I used my battered childhood as an excuse to fall for everything the devil plotted to use against me. Every time I was shown favor and given positive ways forward, I found the easy route was to walk into a different and unique form of sin. Each time God gave me a way, my choice was to follow a devilish path to the easiest means of happiness.

This is/was my real life. I don't need the United States of real women association to come at me with the he is an F-boy anthem nor anyone to scream, "It serves you right," or "That's what you needed," or "What you deserve." Please, by all means, have your reservations about my character, take your time, and please, by all means, if you must, judge me, because I put myself out there in this manner. What I ask is that you be respectful in your judgment as I am not who I was and own my fails. When you find your voice and feel the need to express, don't cast a stone that you wouldn't expect cast at your life. Sin in any capacity is sin in God's eyes, so please, before you place me in a character box, don't judge me by these tales without the full manuscript. You do not know the character of the man I am; you know the faults I have disclosed. There really is so much more to the man; there has to be substance, for how could so many be involved with someone who was really a nobody, as it seems?

I'm not looking for a pity party, no fame socially or personally. This was simply a way for me to dissect and remove many thoughts from inside my head. I know who I am, and I'm very secure with myself. I know all I did, why I did it, when it was done, where it was done at that time it happened. I own it all, yet I sit in tears because I'm human too.

I have traveled through more than just what you have read with the meanest and harshest of instances knocking me over daily. Note, this person wasn't just this person. I wasn't born like this, as the song says. I didn't purposely take advantage of individuals as a way of life or norm as if it was a job or my purpose on this planet. I say all of that to say, this person, well, I'm not just this person; there are many stories and tales of my life which helped create this version of this person. Judge me that's fair. It's okay. I understand. I opened myself up for the judgment, but don't judge me without facts and full understanding into who I really am.

Everyday is a somewhat a repeat of the last. Awake, sad, upset, alone, feel useless, and prepare for tears to appear at any given moment. I let Ratchet out to do his thing, and it's then and only then that I sit completely silent and alone in my thoughts without any distractions. I try to muster up the voice to thank God for breath to life, and most often it's mumbled with the frustration that's the memory of being forced to go to Sunday school, so it's genuine yet it's not.

My apparent anger still is, as I sit in the cologne of pain reminiscing on those days, I joyfully rose out of a king size bed to kiss her lips and whisk her off to her job since I had accomplished what I needed and reached an early retirement. Yeah, nine years older than her but supportive and humble to say I got the house, no worries, bae. I'll clean, I'll cook, do the laundry, walk the dogs, cut the yard, etcetera, and care less what anyone thinks.

I even turned those jobs down like you asked so we can be together. Yeah, I'll not accept a promotion to E9 acting and move to Lemoore, California, with assurance to promote permanent to the same position because you simply said so. All because you said you didn't want me to be away from you. And she said I didn't sacrifice of all sacrifices; I gave up my beloved career.

I hear songs of love, the titles and artists who we know sing of all their hurt and pain. I even have several songs penned throughout my life span which I keep in full rotation. Yes, I am also an artist and have penned more than two hundred fifty songs even recording more than one hundred or so in studio. I recorded several mixtapes and have had my time in the entertainment business opening for some of the most noteworthy acts of my generation while stationed in Pensacola, Florida.

Ironically, I have even recorded songs and videos to accompany the tracks with Lakeisha. I recorded a love song/video in Malaga, Spain, with her and also a breakup song a couple years prior in Virginia during a session at Faith Studios, as if I knew it was to happen. When I go through my catalogue, the sounds remind me of why I have not nor understood why we all seek this thing called love. I listen back and notice my entire life, through song, I was begging for the attention I could never have. I see now that we all grasp for it, even hold it, and all seem to get beaten, battered, and bruised buy it eventually.

"What's Love Got to Do" by the iconic Tina Turner, a song about a woman in a violent relationship she was barely able to escape from. This song is legendary and created the blueprint for several successful theatrical plays and movies. The story of resilience behind the heart and soul of what love could be and the ugliness that it is when handled incorrectly and used improperly to manipulate and control. I often think about the visuals and fear I took advice from the wrong side of the script but also use the flowers in the right moments as I correlate with both sides of this story.

"Real Love" and Mary J. Blige's search for this love, to "What's Love" by Major 9, which became my theme song for the winter of 2020, to the female anthem "Love" and Keyshia Cole, and "Love" by Kendrick Lamar.

Everyday all day next month throughout the year, it's always love, love, love, love, and more love no matter the genre, the time frame, the gender, or race, there is a song about love, and it is normally painful yet painfully real and the truth about how it is and what it is.

My first melodic encounter as I recall my past was Whodini, and it was the future story of my life. I would listen to the album on my parents' record player, and at that time I didn't know I was playing the soundtrack to life. "One love, one love, you're lucky just to have just one love," they would sing in harmony, and then the crew would yell out each letter like it was their last time actually feeling what love felt like:

The L, then a huge reverbed echo.

And the O another huge reverbed echo.

The V, a lower drop in his voice huge reverberating echo.

To the E!

The story they told each sixteen was a perfect script of broken pain and the ugliness I would so often endure. I think with the differences in age she didn't get to hear that song, but I wonder, I wonder what music has left its imprint on her being. What song plays in her head which says go? What song allows her to walk away so effortlessly?

Songs about love have created my life's love poem:

> If it was "Love for Real" (Everlast), she was in why didn't she put her "Love on Top" (Beyonce), why would she leave after her invested time, like it was nothing.
>
> Why wasn't "Love on the Brain" (Rhianna) or why wasn't she in "Love Galore" (Sza), does she "Love Sosa" (Chief Keef) more than me?
>
> I understand you should "Love Yourself" (Justin Bieber) because no one wants to be a "Lovefool" (The Cardigans) on any "Lovely Day" (Bill Withers) we have, but she left me with "Love Scars" (Trippie Redd) from a crazy "Love Scene" (Joe) that's been hidden behind the yellow tape. Now "Love's Train" (The O'Jays) is derailed

and "Love's Lockdown" (Kanye West) begins to serve its life sentence.

Why wouldn't you just "Love me Now" (Tory Lanez) or "Love me Harder" (Ariane Grande). We made a "Love Shack" (The B-52's) into a home together and created a "Love Story" (Taylor Swift), life was shifting but I now see it was towards "Love's End" (Zeadala).

I feel like "Love Lost" (Mac Miller) in all reality for what we assume our efforts afford us. There was no "Fight for Love" (Sault) no more "Looking for Love" (Jaheim), "Love's Dead" (Victoria Kingz) and you will never "Love me Again" (PnB Rock).

I tried to "Love you Better" (Future) knowing that you were my "True Love" (Coldplay) an "Electric Love" (BØRNS), Plus at this stage in life knowing my past issues I felt I was finally "Ready for Love" (India Arie) and ready "To Be Loved" (Lizzo). It makes me think to myself "Could You Be Loved" (Bob Marley). "The Love Scene" (Joe) and "The Love Songs" (Al Green) you play don't show you what "My Love" (The Dream) is.

You will say it's a "Love Game" (Lady Gaga) not where "Love Grows" (Paravi) or remind you of how we could "Love in the Dark" (Adele). I was different and felt the change. My secrets and their secrets decided to run because "Love in the Way" (Yung Bleu) isn't our normal since we left the old soul and their "Love in the Club" (Usher).

I spent so much time working on us reflecting on how all of me was your "Lover Boy" (Mariah Carey) better yet your "Certified Lover Boy" (Drake) as you needed. I hope I can find "Another Love" (Tom Odell) one day. A love to stand by me during my worst and be a force during my best. The "Love Dive" (IVE) you sent me on says "Only Love Can Hurt Like This" (Paloma Faith) ending like I was hit with your "Love Bomb" (N.E.R.D).

"Hate It or Love It" (Game/50 Cent) you will always be the "Love of My Life" (Erykah Badu) and I'll probably never "Fall in Love Again" (Todd Dulaney) "If I Ever Fall in Love" (Shai). I fight to be a better man and a better me, understanding my role, my fault, my intent and realize there is no more, "Crazy in Love" (Beyonce) so I must "Lose You to Love Me" (Selena Gomez) which means pain and suffering on an endless road to "No Love" (Summer Walker) or "Fake Love" (Drake) since "My Love" (Justin Timberlake) slash "Ex-Lover" (Janta) didn't want "This Love" (Maroon 5) or thought maybe I was "Bad at Love" (Halsey).

I don't want to hurt anymore because "We Found Love" (Rihanna). I'll see, because I don't want to "Fall in Love" (Slum Village) again, but regardless your "New Love" (Victoria Monet) "Guess Who Loves You More" (Raheem Devaughn) signed dearly, "Tainted Love" (Soft Cell).

I would will typically follow a good tear session with a Band-Aid of blame finding all the reasons why she doesn't love me so that I could pause my emotions playing back dates and names like footage from old videotapes. Dudes I just knew she slept with appear partly from knowing her past more likely from my own guilt. Maybe it was her real intent to succeed alone in life in promotion and profession, not ever personal, using me as she did her previous guy friend after her abuse from her husband to simply heal her wounds, leaving me to watch her house and dog while she did her naval duties.

Since I have no evidence of any of the above, I am left with wishing that I could find a small stop to me crying. I replace love with hate. I spell them out in bold gold letters like the rings on radio Raheem's knuckles from the Spike Lee joint. I never get a reason that I can just move on. See, it's not enough I wasted years of my life, several days, several hours, many minutes; the time, though most important, was miniscule compared to my pain.

It wasn't the fact I spent a lot of my own throughout in resources, travels, gifts, business ventures and turned down employment to support her dream. Nah, it couldn't stop my pain. The pain of knowing what I did once I felt betrayed. There's no one to console me. I didn't have a girl power group to hear one side of the story I was stuck with the ones who took advantage of me inside the storm. I stood in my pain while confused in my storm knowing it's the best so-called friends and the looks I received behind the closed doors.

It's knowing that all I created and controlled I assumed was gone and without one single explanation as to why. Even knowing she kept one of two rings after I asked if you are done to send it back, and she didn't. She never did.

I was with her when she pawned her wedding rings after divorce, and I saw her evil side. I've seen it firsthand, the switch after the years of issues, but in my head, I often wonder why I didn't get a second chance.

This leads me to believe I was in love, loved hard, and how did I get here, how did I allow my insecurities to place me in such a position? Why was I now at a disadvantage? What was the reason, her real intent? What was the devil's plan? It was perfectly laced out to ensure I could never roam through the walls of another heart in vain again.

I will probably die without any confirmation, and honestly, I'm not okay with it at all but hope to understand. I eventually just say it will all be all right, and this is just what I tell myself.

For some unexplained reason, I see this word *love* and its glorified form sitting on a crested wave of water just like that Hollywood sign high above for all to see and/or admire, but I immediately follow its lettering with words like hurt, passion, pain, regret, false, fake, etcetera. For life, as earlier stated, even throughout this stand, I would say forget love but in the four-letter format instead. It isn't a tangible thing; this love thing can't be real. This world displays the perfect daily examples with killings, murder, death, hate, separation, destruction, blame, assault, and we all live in the same America. A place where its anthem screams love throughout, but its picture isn't one of the same, and if this is love, then why would anyone think or believe any different than I do about it?

If my direction on what love was, what love is, or what it could be was a learned behavior from America, I know damn well I'm doomed as I have been, because America doesn't love, not one bit. I have lived abroad. I know what love in a country looks like, and this isn't it. Maybe, just maybe, one day I can take myself back to Iceland, Sicily, Spain, maybe France, Greece, or Italy—all places I know love does exist. Places I found like. Places where there is love and hearts that beat as one.

It is crazy how the actions prove just, regardless the language barrier and awkward shifts in time and color differences. Maybe this was all scripted, and she is elsewhere. Maybe she was from a distant place, and I limited my search. Maybe this was to be so I can feel a pain so harsh my next love would be placed on a pedestal so high she couldn't escape, or maybe I'm just dreaming.

No longer getting high off medicated sticks perfectly rolled. Daily I would smoke my pain away. Mind shifting on purpose, deep inhales of different strains each and every day going from planet to planet masking my personal issues barely holding it together like duct tape on the repair. And then it all stopped.

For whatever reason, I was moved and scared spiritually out of the smoke to bask not in the essence of herbs but the daily in my face pure essence of pain. An elevated stench of skunk. As it burns like a never-ending roach with no high attached at all, I sit and inhale the truth.

Another day and my cycle's the same. Awake 11:00 a.m. after hoping to sleep the entire morning away here. Feeling like the more time I have awoke, the more hurt I'm forced to feel, so I lay awake at night tranced into television until I whisper words to God which are often, I feel, unheard.

I eventually fall asleep. Typically, the night is interrupted by this dog finding his way into my bed, and this is where he snuggles up against me at times. I wonder if it is because he feels my pain and hears me cry. Or do all dogs really play out life in the same bed of drama they created?

Normally I turn away to find him wondering why as I fight my feelings. I'm not sure I am normal. I yell at him, "Who do you think I am?" in a tone that suggests anger when really, he hasn't done anything other than naturally try to console the person he loves. I would say over and over that God was punishing me for my ways in life. I now have been sent to sleep my life away with this dog she bought night in and night out. My mental health wouldn't allow me to get rid of him or wish him away. He was mine from birth and has been the only party with me this entire time.

Every tear, all the pain, the hopelessness, each and every cross to endure, he has been there; so is he a comfort, simply here to give me insight that even dogs serve a unique and genuine purpose; they have a reason in love. I often dive deep into myself, but this time I simply have accepted my new place and forced myself to walk through this drama.

Two days ago, I thought could you sit in a room of your current thoughts with the pain from your past. Like to sit in a room with the women that you have split energy with. What would that look like? What would it feel like? Aside of the DMX song, what would it sound like?

What did they want from me? I often wondered if it was so wrong, why were they so easy to say yes, what did they think or believe, what was the justification to sleep with the man who was not certifying himself into their futures? Was I inside of an opposing and opposite strategy and looking for love so hard I was blind to the facts?

I had this unique ability to live in all that now had to offer, never being forced to see a future. I spent year after year never getting internal love nor appreciation, and actually, I spent days working two and three jobs at one time to support someone who had, in my eyes and soul, the perfect agenda and way out.

My ex never graduated from high school or anything for that matter. It's not a jab; it's the truth. She was very well taken care of. My guilt, I believe, was the exchange, and so her bag was secured long after her initial descent.

I believe to this day she stuck it out with me because she understood what was at the end of the rainbow regardless of my intent or lack of. I understand the role I played in the entire marriage. I became numb toward my wife, and the outside was the only escape. I used her; abused her mentally, verbally; and took full advantage of the ability to stay, leave, deploy, and seek refuge with other individuals as it became our normal way of life.

I now understand the term two wrongs don't make a right. I found fault in her lack of support, inability to find her place in life, and the excuse that her education or lack of would not allow her to simply be my support or the support I wanted in couple ship. No support, no help, always giving was my excuse and reason to begin to walk in a life with sin.

Was it right? No, it was not, and I understood what I was up against, but for some reason, the words that kept ringing in my head to this day, "You can find love," and if you ask any individual I came across, I would always state what I believed was my truth. I could eventually find real love.

Before the talks of love were spoke on, I would always ensure they knew I would never leave again for anyone until my children were of age. This was wrongly embedded in me as a child. I simply took words my father screamed at me in the calmest of tones and out of context on a life journey without proper clarification and ran with it. Even as I defied those words on a separate occasion I spoke to earlier, it only ensured they were embedded into my head deeper after we were ironically back in the same household. Man, what a setup it was to end right back in the same position after I had been separate for almost three years. And to think it all started twenty years earlier with her lies.

I recall walking into my house after getting the news and telling my mother this was one of the worst days of my life at the time because I didn't know what anyone's reaction would be toward me since I already had several demerits to my name and this was just another one to be added to the list of faults that I carried. The entire situation seemed to be set up in some way, shape, or form. My ex-wife at fifteen years old had a plan.

Ketchup in a maxi pad, wow, a fifteen-year-old female. I'm sure she was scared and lost in her own life. I went into my own shift at the same time but decision that affect lives for life, that's not right. I was forced to grow up, and I saw firsthand very young the manipulated world of a woman's web. How they do what's necessary to get what they want via scheme.

I remember calling and asking her after missed periods because we both tracked her ovulation and taking of the birth control. She would always say she was taking them as prescribed, and as she missed her periods, she would mask her pregnancy with fake cycles to prolong her pregnancy.

Anyways, I understood the cost in my extramarital affairs, so to speak. I never turned my back on my financial obligations, and I made sure the females knew my hurt, fear, and pain. All the others were the ones who I told my every secret and story to. They were the women I cried to at night or called throughout the day. They were the heartbreakers, the chosen ones, actually most often the choosers as my issues normally kept me shamed until approached.

I could never break in but weak when the doors are open and I'm invited. Just as the Proverbs describes of the woman with the open door and foul lips. The realities would cause for those invites, and I would most often accept each, chasing a love close enough to the real thing; it worked for me. But what about the others in the room? I wonder where they sit in this sin. I wonder what could be said aloud amongst the room, what are our soul ties in life, and do the old memories ever cross their minds as we now sit in adulthood at this very moment at this time?

I wonder If any of them ever really loved me as they said. What was the true expectation from our actions? Do they see each other as they do is their blame? There isn't any confusion, no crazy TV episode fallouts; I simply see me sitting surrounded by the years of lust, love, ignorant choices, and pain all reaching and reciprocating a return, but I don't have any arms.

Meaning I finally had my one who I gave my all to, and so to move forward in life means that finally I need to be okay with knowing the room which once had guest on its list is now one I sit alone in.

No memory of late nights and wrestling in beds to achieve satisfaction momentarily. No memoirs of dinners and dates, trips and travels abroad thanks to our profession. The calls, compliments, the stress, and conversation. Matching outfits and club crashes new reminders of commitments via photo and the sounds of each individual voice.

I now sit knowing in order for me to properly move forward, I must take this time to remove those thoughts of a life in my past. Carrying each into a new journey only means my back as I awake shall stay the same—as dirty as it's ever been.

I wonder!

Could this be her coping skill? Could this be how my ex-fiancé is able to cut me off like unpaid city water and move on to the next? Well, if so, I bet the conversation in her room is completely different.

Really, I wish that conversation was intimately only with me and the erasing allowed us to move forward in rare form as Will Smith and Tommy Lee (*MIB*) would just snap their fingers in our faces from behind the watchful eyes of the all-black Ray-Bans, and this nightmare I've lived would innocently enough be removed, and I move forward.

Guess for now I'll wishfully think and live with my regrets. Both what it is and feelings that push me to a place midday I hate, and that's already into tomorrow, and I've only been awake an hour and a half. Could this be it, be my full-time life from here on out sleeping to wake with questions to sleep and repeat? Who knows, but I can honestly say that as I go throughout each moment and learn more about myself, I get stronger not only in self but closer to God.

I wonder, was this all to happen on purpose because of the man that I was creating to be not the man that I was created to be?

I believe God gives us a leash, and He allows us to walk through our life, make difficult decisions on our own, and in His grand scheme of things He sees fault and allows us to deviate from a righteous path ever so slightly before we are pushed into format again to follow our path toward destiny.

The issue is when you are so far away from your faith you do not have an understanding as to what is happening to you when it happens and why it happens, and all you feel is what you currently endure. Typically, in instances such as mine, you find yourself on the back end of a force which now has to reestablish you in life for what your original purpose was.

God has a plan for us all, and when we deviate from his plan, there are hiccups that are placed along life's journey which ultimately affect someone else down the line. This is that humongous puzzle with a billion pieces which all need to interact in a specific way at a given time.

When those pieces don't find their way to their proper spaces, there needs to be an outside force to realign what needs to happen, when it needs to happen, how it should happen, so that we all can maneuver in what our God-given purpose is. It is then and only then that we can live a proper and level lifestyle.

My Past, Introduced
To Today's Insecurities!

Trying and find a sense of normal, I took my classmate's wife up on her invite. Her husband Omar's fiftieth birthday party was over Halloween weekend, and a month earlier I saw him at the same reunion party I saw Sharee at. Omar and I actually have a unique history. You see, he and I are cut from the same cloth. We both lived on the same side of the city and have had our share of youthful growing pains. We used to walk home at times and wonder what was so uniquely different about us which made us walk the fine line at fitting in. He and I both fans of childish things as young adults such as karate flicks and comic books. The things you dare not speak about at school amongst a group who was into so many adultlike things. Dare I speak about my infatuation with the X-men or He-Man, but I cherished our conversations because they were some of the only times in my life I could really be who I was without judgment.

We would stop at the local arcade on our walks, and if we had a few quarters, we would go back and forth at the latest video offerings until we were out of funds and then make our way on, just enjoying the youthful nature of life. He was one I always had favor for because he was a safe space outside of my silence. I never had to create a being as I was me, and that was cool enough for him, and that was reciprocated. He wasn't the funny guy with the Kwame haircut; he was just ODD, a name I called him which eventually stuck.

He was one who I believe was transitioning through some of the exact same obstacles and challenges, so it was okay to confide in

122

him how my childhood likes I still carried into high school as he was etching the characters in private at that same time. We carried the same values in family and friends, and so a unique ship was formed that I have always ensured I kept solid even in our distance as I grew in the military.

Omar knew the ills of the inner city and somehow, someway was able to maneuver around the funk as he got into the basketball team's success, and I ventured into my journey with the baseball team.

This is where we would find a normal separation in the class because our places in the social structure changed. He was now a bit more in the in crowd as basketball player as the sport carried more status in inner city social circles versus the predominately unknown vices of the baseball diamond.

It was to neither of our faults; it is just how life happens as you grow into who your destined to be, so I never faulted him for the change in life, but I actually was excited to see that the things we would complain or discuss ion the confines of our own conversations would now be a memory in his mind as he was now able to be around those who we once looked at from the outside.

Honestly, I believe to this day he would wish he could just be him as he stuck to his morals and ethics and never got overly consumed with that side of the track as he is and has always been simply O, and that is a testament to his character which was another reason why I decided to seize the moment and take his wife up on her invite to his surprise birthday party.

It took everything in my power to get the nerve up to go since I had been in the midst of the most horrific year of my existence, but I did it not for myself but to pay respect to one who had went out of his way to attend my retirement ceremony after twenty-six years of me being gone. Shelby Davis, Tiffany Ross, William Tindle, and O all made reservations to attend my day and celebrate the fact that I made it out the hood and was able to accomplish a feat most of us don't, and that meant and means the world to me. The least I could do is suck up my feelings and show him the same support as this is what love is.

Once I got my mind made up that I would attend, I asked Sharee if she would like to attend the party as well since she was cool with him, and she was at the time again doing me a favor and letting me stay on her property in my travel trailer until my next move somewhere.

By now I settled mentally on no physical activity as I placed her into a box, so I was cool. I, as a token of my appreciation for the stay, told her I had no issue with paying for her flight to offset my stay if she wanted to attend.

I reached out to his wife and asked to have a plus one, and it was set. We were now going to Saint Louis in support of an old friend. In my thinking, I am feeling accomplished a bit in my spiritual movement as I am abiding by all these rules which I avoided most my life, but this is all off and awkward. I feel unlike myself as every single movement I question as if one mistake would set me back in life to day one like this was an initiation of some sort God had me on.

I felt like every thought I had or moment in the day was watched by the spirit and that I was in supreme judgment for my life. I was under the microscope, so to speak, and it made me stress and have severe anxiety for who can avoid anything from the hand of God.

Crying off and on the week leading up, I again began to feel awkward. I started to have extreme reservations about traveling with her because the only person I've flown with in the last seven years was the shadow I've been in love with, so in hindsight, I pre-planned my intent.

I was so in my own thoughts about my ex that I was losing myself day in and day out the closer it got to the date of travel. I had a preconceived notion that it would be fine because we could fly separate as in same time, same flight but get it how we live. In conversation, she stated candidly, "I'm excited, and thanks for the invite. Also, did you seat us next to each other, because I want to fly with you." I obliged during the order, but mentally I already knew it was going to be an emotional trigger for me. Her intent, as pure as it was, it was becoming a major downfall for my weekend. Sad part is that she would never even know it.

As the time to leave grew closer, she asked if it was cool to stay in my hotel room since she hadn't spoken with her extended family or friends. Her request, as genuine as it was, because she was nowhere the person I was and probably didn't think it was an issue, didn't know the demons I fought with daily just being LeRon. I thought to myself, God, why test me like this and place me in these positions? It isn't about the moment; it is about me and a lifetime full of enjoying the moments with like-minded individuals. This was nothing like those moments; this felt like her footsteps were ordered and my position was to play my role taking my medicine in hopes to fight the inner demons I have carried a lifetime as crutches.

Being in a transformation, I took this as an opportunity to be a better force, so just to make things convenient and for cost issues, I said no worries; I can get two queen size beds. Then it hit me that Friday. *LeRon, what are you doing? This truly is an issue for you know how you moved.*

Sharing my personal space, this was not my way. I've never done this on purpose, yet the okay was already spoken. Typically, when I traveled with someone and we knew our places in each other's life, I ensured we had our own spaces, for who knows what may happen while on a vacation.

Things were significantly different now. I was not living high off the hog as years before. I am homeless or RVing, so the funds once used to do are no more; my financial situation surely wouldn't allow me to do what I normally would. I just can't afford to assist a friend with their own accommodations without putting myself in jeopardy with future obligations as I was traveling to Pensacola, Florida, upon our return.

This here led to a trigger which the night before begins to boil over. All I thought of was how not only was I in flight with her but how now at my most weak physical lack and mental pain, I was playing roommate with one of God's chosen. I felt like I was being chaperoned to the dance by God's chosen one.

Her youngest daughter picked up my puppy, which was always the original plan before her even going. I felt sideways because he is my security blanket at this point in my life and the entire year I had not separated from his side while I dealt. I didn't get to say goodbye to him since I had to scramble to get a last-minute haircut. This in turn set my attitude off on my left yawl, and I was in a negative mood for sure.

Who am I to complain when I already feel like a freeloader? was my thinking.

That night before the travels was different inside her home, we talked and talked a lot with her family and openly about spirituality, which is the norm here.

I think I did so much rambling and pushed limits not only because of the alcohol I decided to out the blue consume but out of anger since I missed my ex, and here, I was about to travel and crash with the most holy person I knew at that time.

You better get it together because you're going on a field trip with one of God's true angels, and this is a spiritual test, I would remind myself. Fact is, I had the opportunity to be with a woman in Saint Louis over this weekend, someone that I knew very well. She had recently shown a lot of interest in me, and we had already communicated, and the scene was intimately set from weeks earlier via conversation out the blue.

I believed that this new change in events was to ensure I didn't get to the hotel and in one weekend make the choice I believe I really wanted to, and that was to bed someone since I felt so alone. I could have put a Band-Aid on my pain with someone who I know thinks of me in a good way, as a good man. She expressed how much she felt that I was a good man and that she could see me in her future life. I wasn't jumping into a future, but as a man and one who was love-struck to know that even now as I am at my lowest still had a chance to be with one who saw favor in me excited my opportunity to move as I did at one time. Those words in my weakest state allowed me to feel some sense of normal, or at least like the man I was.

That night prior we talked off and on about God and His plan for His people, the whys and why nots. I often became angry and combative and even cried between lustful eyes as the feeling of the devil was there. Tainted thoughts presented themselves often, and then the energy shifted as her son offered an amazing prayer over myself his older sister and her friend.

It was a unique power in his voice and tone. I watched as everyone in the room got extremely emotional holding on to his every word of encouragement and support for a better tomorrow. And me, I had thoughts going in a million directions a wide range from several places inside my soul. I was being moved, and the shift was an inner battle with right and wrong, the good and bad, the gift and curse, and all the struggles in my life. The thing I would break concentration on would be when he spoke in tongues.

This sent me off at times and to other places, for that was new in my freshly acquired spiritual life, and it just weakened my vibe. I don't know if it's an excuse or the sinner in me feeling unworthy to be in their circle of praise. Me feeling like my past was so heavy I was being mocked for the issues, and I needed that much more help, but once again it was me in my head. Why hadn't my parents who I know for a fact were more into their walk do this? My grandparents never gave me these ritualistic vibes, the church never presented this tone, and now I was in a full-fledged crash course inside someone else's praise, so yes, I was off.

I get confused when I hear the rambling of words and tongue, for I grew up around those who prayed power into your life via the Lord without that need, so without a judging ear, my thoughts roamed thinking about both good and bad things, finding my moments to listen and connect good vibes and happy reservations at the same time.

My reservations were not about his prayer or the sincerity of it but of myself and my thoughts, my actions in front of God as I stood. This became a stalemate, and after seeing his sister break completely down and the family friend do the same, both releasing some severe inner pain and stress, I knew it was a healing. I just questioned, why didn't I crack in my stance like the rest? Why didn't I bow and cry and praise or feel moved to their level of emotion?

I left feeling good but awkward at the same time and knew then the weekend ahead was necessary or going to mentally kill me.

I slept for a few hours then arose with an attitude like it's planned, and the sooner we go, the faster I cry, and we return with my same dirty back, and then, we were off.

We rushed to her planned speaking engagement. She was giving a poetic presentation to women who were victims of domestic violence and had to go through the trauma of abuse. It was October and a great cause to help break the cycle. Her being one who overcame those trials and tribulations was a great addition to their panel, I believe.

On our ride there, I sat thinking of my own interactions with verbal onslaughts and the fights that were my past. The issues that couples undergo and where it leaves both parties. I said, man, it's amazing how women really band together and support each other. My mind is in a blur, and I was wondering why men, especially of my hue, are America's lowest commodity.

I won't go deep into my thought on this subject here, but I really do see how Black men are now soon to be extinct even in our own communities. I see how I played into the stereotype and how I am glad I was able to reroute my children's route in this life.

In my emotions, I sat in her car wondering what I am doing while she completed her task. My mind raced, and I needed calming, so I began to listen to the Bible. Though it gave me a moment of peace, I also start the same questioning, wondering, why am I at my low, why does it feel like death upon me, why did I do this, why did I do that, and most importantly, am I even loved? This is my daily struggle often feeling forsaken to be a nobody because in the blink of an eye, my everything was gone.

I was now the low. The one without no one to lean on or cry to. All I had was my thoughts, my faith, and Ratchet. I press forward telling myself I will be fine, and then I snapped out of it as she walked out.

See, Sharee is a happy-in-the-now spirit, and she simply spoke about flying together, rooming together, transiting together, and even matching for the party. This was what I did with my ex, and I surely wasn't with her. I was traveling respectfully with the one I considered holy and full of spirit and, even more so in my mind, another test into my future.

Why and I mean how could I do all this with a person I barely knew personally aside social media and our high school days, let alone someone I didn't have my normal connection with? We weren't even in how I view the word, real friends. This all was so spur of the moment and out of line with my normal planning and way of life.

We get to our flight, and the entire time I am in a bad place. Attitude, pouting, and dismayed. The forces were boiling inside, and I snapped. On the flight, when asked if anyone wanted to move to open seats upfront, I offered, and as the attendant asks if we are together, I said quickly no, and she said yes. This burned my insides to flame, and I angrily yelled no then turning to her to state the same, "Listen, we aren't together." Tension was immediately felt. It came from a place of hurt and out of nowhere. I was humiliated by my actions and immediately felt the tension and uneasiness as warranted.

Our row mate got the move; that was crazy in itself as he was flying with his wife and two very dysfunctional children. I understand why he wanted out; he was looking to escape the noise and fighting, leaving his wife to suffer alone from the rear of us. He swiftly departed, and I shifted one seat over, and it was then I felt bad for snapping, but I was now fully established in my role with her moving forward.

We got to the hotel after zero conversation, dressed, and attended the function, which was an amazing event and worth the travels. Upon arriving back to the hotel, sleep was in order, and I slept all day Sunday on purpose hoping the return trip would hurry on to be, but that night, while lying in my bed listening to her sleep, I got emotional, and it hit me hard.

Being in a hotel and all to myself alone in my bed simply recalling all of the years of traveling around the world with Lakeisha hit my soul. When I say I gave in and the emotions were so over me, I mean I started to feel an emotional outpouring that was not normal. I immediately got up so that I wouldn't be heard, and I went to the gym and worked out and cried the entire time. Actually, to be honest, the tears started under my covers.

I went to the gym and cried so I wouldn't be heard by Sharee. This was sickening since I truly don't get why I simply can't walk away from my past relationship. Why was I being forced to carry this pain so long? I prayed and pleaded, I begged and changed, so why am I still forced to reflect on the one thing I feel is holding me back from moving forward?

Why is it that she can throw the memory of me away and work on in life without a flaw? What made her so strong and able to just let go from everything established unlike myself? I feel like I am damned, and the karma is the turn of every day being reminded of my life's investment and how it crashed to a no more.

I felt like a walking mistake, like the entire world was laughing at me right in front of my face. I try to mask my hurt with the gym, but after it's all done, I truly felt alone, and it hurts even more that I was in the form I knew. The hurt was increased by the fact I assumed by now God had a hand on my life, and this was a mirror of the moments when as a child I would blame Him for the troubles I endured as a kid.

I wondered if this was a mental challenge to see how far I had come. I still got mad and upset at the why vice being give instruction so I could move on in life and do what I was supposed to, but the life I was living didn't mean it was readily accessible information. I still didn't get it. I was dibbling and dabbling in the reading of the Bible but not committed because it was easier to blame.

I jump in the shower and wash away the hurt and pain, letting my tears fall with the water as if I'm hiding my emotions from the world, but in all reality it's in me; I feel each one of them fall and run down my face individually from the shower water, sniffling and snorting like a child who has had his favorite toys taken away. I hate this feeling; I hate the way I am being moved and all that is being asked; I hate the challenge of incompletion and being put in time-out, a time-out that right now has been a year, but it actually to me seems like a lifetime.

There in my mind right now is a let-go that needs to happen. The biggest question is how. There is no going back, LeRon. Get out your damn head and let her go as she has moved on and promoted. How do I know? Well, I lay in silence and looked at promotions from the Navy. Why? I don't know, probably hoping to see her achieve. I mean I was there from the beginning and felt invested as I helped write and rewrite papers and package information. I was with her during the workouts and the baby challenge. I threw the promotion party and was the guest speaker at the ceremony. I was there during COVID at her schooling by her side as she achieved. I went to her graduation in Rhode Island and supported her efforts, and to think I was told I didn't support—go figure, right?

The other reason was evil since I was displaced like rubbish. I also hoped in the same breath that she was a failure, and God was punishing her for how she treated me. I hoped not to see her excel and that she was also being sent on an emotional joyride like I was. I wanted to see that she was going through the pain as I was in this situation. To see that she was alone and hurting probably with her decision.

Then it hit me. My eyes were blurred, and there it was. I saw her promoted to CWO3 all while I lay in the bed alone, lifeless, and without. I broke down into a rainstorm. How could this be, God? You know what it is and what it was, God. You watched me, and all I gave and how my side of the story was also bent and controlled. You know what I gave and lost, and she was winning. Really, God? This blew my mind. This in my head simply reassured me that I was the real issue; I was the bad guy, the venom, and virus; and it was then I gave in.

A homeless soul who once sat at her table as the king was not even in a thought as her life progressed, and as I wondered, what about me? I once again slipped into a sad mind space which blaming myself was the only action that morning after the normal arise and cry. I left for the gym to finish the tears eventually running out and giving in to what's my reality.

Truth be told, I never was taught love, the real language or emotion. I never knew what love felt like or looked like. I always played defense, and now, right now, as I sit with my daily reminders of what my chance at love was, I feel disgusted at my actions and my view since I ruined my chance at real love by doing what I learned, and that was protecting myself from what I have ended up feeling right now.

The believing she would never love me how I loved her and that I needed to keep souls around for when she left me. Even though I know my mistake, it's so hard to view it in a better manner. Never had I made my lifestyle my normal. I lied by not talking about the things which were important to me and that I use women to mask my real fears.

I let having female friends and bed partners be my grace and safe place which left holes and gaps in my home. I can never get her to say certain things which gave me the excuse to be unfaithful after she left for Spain the final time. It was at that moment after a visit home she lay in a bed and shouldn't bear to be physical with me. She would look at me with a face that shown she was trying to get by. In my head, I wondered who travels all this way and shows no affection, none at all.

What in the world happened to us was my mind state. This was all before the above trip, and it was then I was moved to leave her home and venture out on my own; I still don't know why I left to this day. It was something inside my head which was guiding me. I listen to spiritual leaders and how they say God will move you when He decides it is time to get you away from the vices you are clinging to, and I can only assume this was when my journey began to take fold in real life.

I gave me the okay to sleep with others. My mind said she has tormented you and left you to burn with no explanation, no conversation, and or reason, so do you. Reality was, I never wanted to do anything. I was hurt, tired of the crying and being alone, tired of her coming in and out of my life for the past twenty months with zero explanation. It was simply what I knew to do to spare myself from being lonely. And in the end, the part that hurts me ten times over now is she left me, and I don't have anyone I kept around for reasons as originally planned.

I don't even have those who were there while I was waiting for that moment. How ironic my social life has been completely removed. Phone numbers and contacts gone, no way to reach the vices I used for years. I see it all unfold, left to wonder what was it all for from the jump. Why had I set myself up for a complete failure and have to literally face this fact day in and day out? How could I now believe that my learned behavior, lust for women, fear of loneliness, narcissism, and belief that I had it in control, trying to buy time until I said I do at the alter would work?

I pray for correction, for now all I have left to lean on is hope. I hope I'm not considered a lost cause, a demon or hell-bound soul because of my sins. I love God too much; I have a faith that's pure; I care about others, give freely my all; and I believe in His hands because I've been covered my entire life. Could the spiritual world see my character flaws and continued damage I would place on others so the spiral was necessary to save lives, especially hers?

I wonder, was the divine realm behind my demise and saving in unison? If so, my question was and is, will I ever find love, or is this who I am to be? From where I sit now, I know if I am allowed to love again, she would never, ever need to worry about who I am, where I'm at in our relationship, or how I feel.

Being alone is different from silence. Alone makes you look at others in love with the blinded eye, somewhat jealous and envious. You also believe in their stories that there's hope for you. You hope eventually you're given the chance to do it the right way, no secrets, no plans, no protecting personal assets or emotions, no interruptions from the outside, just you and her, one-on-one, with the greatest help from God, whoever she may possibly be.

You live by His code, walking together happy into the next life both knowing through the good and bad you got someone to wash your back anytime, all the time, and this to me is the picture of what love should be.

Not perfection or without flaws or dysfunction but the knowing and building of a thing so great the noise from outside is like flies; you simply swat them away and keep moving forward together as one. Ja Rule said love is pain, and now, I get what was meant. Love is pain and so many other words wrapped into one, but when you're without love, all you know and feel is the pain of it.

You sit daily in your sins looking back at all the yesterday's saying I wish I knew this was going to be my love because if I knew, I would have treated her with the utmost respect in life and loved her and her only, for even a blind man must eat though he knows not what's on the menu by sight. He has faith it will quench his hunger, and the love I didn't know I had I now know provided all the nourishment I needed.

Alone and hungry I sit knowing I'm ready for my next her, emotionally and mentally, but the past drama has created new hurdles, so I sit sad and prayerful one day God will see fit to bless me again.

Sharee, I am sorry for the rollercoaster ride I pulled you on. I'm battling myself, and I'm glad my bipolar chain of events didn't ruin a good friendship. The above is much you didn't know transpired as it was my fight and not yours to have to deal with even though I believe you knew there was an issue with my spirit. I hate how I behaved and regret allowing myself to come out of character as well.

I want you to know that your spiritual guidance has been amazing, and I thank you for understanding me and the journey I'm on. I hold you in high regard as a person and will always be indebted to you for your undying support while I figure life out. I thank you very much!

*****

I have now transited on and sit in Pensacola, Florida. The funny thing is I believe this year's journey has taken me to all the places and destinations that I set foot in while active duty and creating this storm. I have caused grave emotional damage leaving a trail of soul ties around the globe, whether lifelong or momentarily. The root of all the scars starts and ends with a tie to me.

The year 2022 started with me being reckless, and it is ending with me feeling every sign of regret that I could possibly feel. All of the deceit, lies, and history are buried in cities within these states, or they hold claim to the lives of those I've come across.

Each place I've visited I look back on situations. I was forced to see places and feel things I thought I had let go. Each place caused me to feel a unique emotion as I had to go through the why, the whats, and whos that were involved picturing the now of the lives that are impacted, some positive and some negative. It really takes a lot out of you and is draining. I can't believe this was a lifestyle carrying this baggage around for years. I can't believe I am sane; it really makes you wonder.

I understand the temptations that fall upon me especially as I sit now isolated at the water knowing that with one phone call, I could possibly fall back into that web of darkness.

I don't. I refuse to allow my history to create my story if there is an opportunity for it to be rewritten in a positive light. I can only pray as I walk in my truth, hoping I can see things for what they really are and not for what I want them to be.

I can understand better my role in life's puzzle and how patience is key to ultimately find my position. As I close this moment in time, I am empty and left to wonder, if we are love and created in His image, why is a life built on love so hard to live?

You write page after page, releasing thought after thought. It is placed on the pad and you hope to clear space. You hope you remove the clutter out your mind for new passages. I pray that with clarity and better understanding finally comes ownership, and this owner-ship becomes the eraser for my guilt and pain.

This presentation was never meant to be strictly about my lack of love or my desperate need for love. It isn't about my current want of a love I seem too so desperately long for. It wasn't about the whos throughout the entire journey that played parts along a very devilish role throughout my life. It hasn't been about my journey nor the destinations I currently sit at.

I come to know this was a full-scale onslaught on me getting to know exactly each part I personally play and have played in the feeling I currently possess. It's knowing that blame cannot be placed for what you lack or loss. It's taking ownership of each and every part self-played. No fingers pointed or excuses, simply owning my issues and without blame dealing with the fact that I carry my dirt on my back because I created it, so it's mine to wash for now.

Four months into what has felt like the end of my life, slowly I am able to put small pieces together and reflect on things in a peace which is unique. Currently I am at my bottom, and though I strug-gle daily, I believe the worst is behind me as long as I make decisions which have a positive impact on the days as they go by. I think of all that has transpired around me as of late, and I wonder, why is life made so difficult by all who live it?

I took time out of each of the days given to search for blame vice taking the time to better myself as a person. The hatred in this place is so intense it becomes a part of who you are to the point that it consumes you. The paranoid outburst is a part of the equation which never allows one to find inner peace.

After nights of struggling with myself, I was shaken into a fear which forced me to choose my life or death. Months had passed, and I received a text from Lakeisha out the blue. This was a major setback, though inviting. I took it as the devil trying to have his way with my mind once again. I jumped in my reply not taking into account the recent text I sent that went unanswered.

My selfish side hoped she was coming around, willing to have me return as if nothing transpired. We would discuss the issues and get back to life as normal since she was now back in the States working. Boy, was I in for a rude awakening. She wished me a happy Thanksgiving; this was odd to me as it was truly out the blue. Why would she do this to me? I asked myself. Paranoid, I said she is playing a mind game with me just because she can.

My mind is and has been so messed up I couldn't even accept a simple text without going into a spiral of emotions. I truly let this woman have full control over who I was, and I didn't even know it. Never had I ever had these types of mixed emotions, and I have been in some of the most ridiculous situations. She was the puppet master and in control; pull the string and watch him go, I thought.

She did say she wanted to be friends, but what friend would do what she has done? Who am I to ask that when I have done things that a friend wouldn't do because their feelings got hurt. I went into damage control mode and spoke about how I was in tears most nights and that I wished her well in her new way of life, all to get no reply. This shook me as I wondered, why would she reach out in the first place, why send a text to one you wanted nothing more to do with?

I suffered a couple weeks more before leaving for where I now sit currently in Biloxi, Mississippi, near Kessler Air Force Base. I have been here for a few weeks now; the weather has taken a full turn. I went back in to a dark place and had several thoughts of the afterlife. I asked God why for several nights face full of sludge, and then I just said it: if it is to be this way, why not just take me away from here? I am tired of this back and forth, so please just take me so I can be.

At that moment, I really didn't truly understand the weight of the words I spoke and how sometimes when you ask, God is that much more obliged to show you who He is in real life format. This was December 14th if I am not mistaken and ironically a night I will not forget. There were news flashes about a wintery mix coming from the west and how it was soon going to engulf the States and all the lower forty-right would be affected in some way, shape, or form.

I have been isolated for the last five months, so to me I didn't care about what was going on in the outside world, for I was in my own living nightmare, so the outside at this time didn't matter. I truly didn't care. The temps begin to drop, and the people here were taking the days in as if they were the same. A few days prior, another text that Sunday showed up from Lakeisha shortly after I got the nerve to watch a show on my own; it was called *Cherish the Day*.

For weeks upon weeks, I kept seeing the commercials for the show, and my subconscious was locked in on it, but I would never watch it as I just knew it was a piece of puzzle I was missing. I saved it on my list of things to eventually get to and simply avoided it for a long time. I dreaded watching it because it was some love show, and I knew it would take me into a darken moment, so I reluctantly fought my instincts and gave in.

The plot was two individuals who were high school loves that went twenty-five years apart before stumbling back into each other's lives. The Saturday night episode took me to tears as the song Lakeisha would often sing to me was played in the background of an intimate scene. Jhene Aiko, her voice that of a dove and the woman I was so infatuated, sang a tune that my now ex would sing to me about a forever and how we would follow each other to the farthest places on the earth if just to be with each other.

This was a moment I sat and had to just wonder, why was this the time? I cried after turning it off immediately and woke to a text. The text was that Sunday, and it said basically she wanted to have a conversation. I had mixed emotions and assumed the best and then the worst all to be confronted with the statement that she was wanting to move the rest of my belongings into a storage. I was crushed and spent the next twenty minutes on the phone line crying like a baby exuding every known emotion to man and with her not letting one moment of regret or an inch of compassion away.

She was stone-cold in her tone, and this I knew was the moment that I had to find a way out of it all before I drove myself to death in it. In love with a force to kill every soul tie I had towed along. I asked for death over and over, and then this is where it got real. The storms which were heading to the States arrived and no sooner than I got myself situated they hit. Louisiana was attacked by several tornados, and I dug into my seat saying this is it, and if it is, well, so be it. The alarms started to ring aloud. I was still stubborn and sitting in the trailer as if this wasn't real life. I turned the news on, and soon after the park was notified that each member should seek refuge in the large bathrooms for safety. Ignorantly, I fought it as if I knew nothing would take place, stubbornly sitting and looking at Ratchet like if it is our time to go, then so be it since I have nothing more to live for.

The clouds vanished, and the rain began to drop like missiles. The wind screamed, and the trees began to applaud in the swirl of nature. I thought maybe I could run to my truck and just drive, so I hopped in, dog in hand, and drove in a circle only to end right back up where I started. I got out, went back into the trailer, and things started to rock.

I got scared. It was as if I played a childish game of double dare with the Most High and He was calling my bluff. I quickly decided to go into shelter as they requested. After sitting inside for about an hour, I looked on the phone to catch the news, and it said we were clear. To me this was just another storm that happened to pass by. Mind you I had been in several storms in my life—hurricanes galore, blizzards, floods, and etc.—but never a tornado. This would be the first.

I went into my travel trailer and, with hesitation, finished watching the show till the end actually, if I recall correct, highly upset. I was upset that in the end, they found love and got back together, for

I wanted the story to end as my life had. I guess, just to make things a bit more equal for my real life's sake. I dozed off, challenged, but yet off to sleep I went.

That was an early night, and the next day's routine was at hand. I arose and headed out to walk Ratchet as normal. To my surprise, I overheard the neighbors talking about the destruction and all the damage done in our immediate area. Several RVs and travel trailers had damage, and trees were thrown like branches de-rooted from the soil and placed on their sides like fallen bowling pins. The area was torn.

I walked the park we would hike through daily, and it was a war zone. Power lines down everywhere, the courts broken, and benches slung like frisbees. Debris all over the place and city workers already out to perform the cleanup. I thought to myself, what did I miss, what really happened here? I didn't even think there was a problem, let alone this much damage. I found out later the tornado touched down right in our area and moved north from us as I was on my way to the shelter. It ran a course right through our location and up through Mississippi north of I-10 toward the next city leaving miles and miles of damage along its way.

I sat in silence wondering to myself, was this God Himself ensuring that I knew He heard me and was there with me watching all the while? Was God there and paying attention to my cries, let alone all the angst, and upset I would display with spirituality and why I was in the position I was in? Was God telling me to be mindful of what you ask for because everyone doesn't always get the opportunity to have a second chance such as myself?

I am slowly taking this in as each day after has been a serious wake-up call to what I am and who I am as I sit. How do you want to be remembered? The sad thing as I type this is if I would have been taken, there is not a person who currently knows where I am. I would have been gone without anyone even knowing I was gone, no loved ones, no family, no friends. This to me is the worst way to die, to leave this earth after having given so much to it without anyone even caring.

I now have another struggle to tow. Who wants to die alone? Death is inevitable, but I now know that when you ask for it, please be sure that you are ready, for I know that I wasn't as I look back. Even though my life may not be the reflection of what it once was, it is mine, and I still hope to have enough of it to live in the future to erase the dark moments I lived of it in the past.

I hope that in life I can find a place to settle and work my time out to correct my despair. I don't want to run the world anymore; I just want to control my piece of the pie in it. If that is to find stability and do my best each day to be a model citizen, then so be it, but at least I would have the chance to give and receive for the fruits of my labor.

There is too much hatred going on in 2022 for me to keep beating myself up over the milk that was spoiled years prior. I get it now. I cannot control the love, just like I cannot control several things which happen in life, but what I can control is how I look at each day. Each day is going to be an ongoing struggle, but I am tempting to find the rainbow no matter how bleak it may be. If the sky shows me favor, then I am going to shoot for the stars until I am blessed. We all do not get the number of chances in life that I believe I have gotten, for most those opportunities are slim to none.

I know that I have been shown favor time and time again, and this was one more blessing I can say as I watched the homeless huddle after leaving the gym. That could have easily been me. I could have easily been subject to a lesser form of living in the blink of an eye, and then what? More tears and more complaints about whatnot, when I could've been more appreciative of what then.

So yes, I am downgraded, and I am uniquely at a disadvantage if you compare me now to my then, but when you have life to live, what is a disadvantage but a chance to grow into something better than your before. What is the challenge if you have an opportunity, that is more than a lot of people in this life can say they have. An opportunity and chance to do it again and even better this time around.

I feel bipolar as I write tonight, and if it is so, then maybe this is the me I need to hang out with more often. One who sees the beauty in a struggle without the teary-eyed, slobber-filled mouth full of complaints about moments that I should just let go of. God will make it all work as I know He has not brought me this far to simply toss me away; there have been to many opportunities to allow for me to be taken. I am here for a purpose, I have worth, and there is something brewing. What it is, who knows but God. I will try to hold steadfast in my faith and continue to study and appreciate life as it is until I am given chance to prove my worth for what destiny may be. Until then, I will sit and have my emotional struggles alone. I am human and fight to stay sane.

God knows who played what roles in the drama of my life. He knows who was in on the shams. He knows my parts and the parts of others, so if anyone will be placed in correction, let it be him who corrects, not me. I own my sin just as the next shall eventually own theirs.

His will, maybe one day we all will reside in harmony as one once we all understand that love, yes, it is needed and so very necessary, but love, unless it is right, will never be the key to any happiness without faith in God ensuring that the love is right.

*****

December twenty-fifth is among us, and as I sit in anger watching the entire world monetize a day which was supposed to celebrate the birth of Christ. I wonder, how did we get here? I wonder, how did we go from honoring the Son of the Father, which was what I was taught, to worrying about the gifts we were to receive?

Where was humanity going as society has completely changed what once was a sacred day to it being the spectacle of spending it now is? We spend so much time on who gets what and what we expect, vice the day that was given us a savior to allow us to even be in the way we are as sinners.

God, for reason on a unique day, sent his only begotten son to us to celebrate in a second chance at life, not for us as a reason to gift or celebrate self.

We have not in total shown a definite level of respect for the offering He was to who we are to be as a people, so to celebrate as if we have come so far is ludicrous. It baffles me how man has for centuries changed the way we were to see God and His gifts to control and manipulate the people. From the irony of so many things to the continued support and praise for those who use God and spirituality as a basis to manipulate and cause destruction amongst his people.

If we all are His children, I believe it matters not where you are from or how you speak. It matters not what you have or the lack of the same. It is not the power to control and ability to take advantage of His people for your own will. How can men and women, who are in power, use scriptures to divide and separate us as God's children?

We were made to uniquely be a bigger piece to his ultimate picture, all made different on purpose, to bring so many alternate concepts and ways forward in a large melting pot of what love was to be. We as people continue to fail as we seek to have control of something the spiritual world will not relinquish.

What is a leader if he is to lead no one and live alone? Leaders use the word of God to bring weakened spirits in to follow them, but not one is using the word to ultimately bring us all to a place where we can live amongst each other as intended.

The wars reign on for control of land that no one owns. They fight for control of what God blessed us with, in hopes that they may harness more control over the world in whole. What happens next? What happens when you believe that you are the master, when you feel that you are so in control of man that God decides to do what He did once before? What happens when God decides to rid the earth from this ugliness and start again as He did once before?

I fear that if we do not soon find a way to live harmoniously amongst each other, God will find reason to ensure what he originally planned will be followed through with a new set of loved ones. He did it once, so what's stopping Him from doing it again? The world as we know it is being destroyed. Storm after storm and natural disasters are wreaking havoc over the world. We are now being forced inside to think about our actions, and yet we only find peace behind technological advances which separate us further.

When does it all end? When can we find love as a whole? Here I am looking for love in life, and yet the examples of love around me are pictures of death and continued destruction, so how is it I can assume there is ever to be love when I do not believe love even exist in a society that has for eons been ugly, cold, and vindictive?

The temperature has dropped like it has an intense reason to wreak havoc; I have a sense it is for a purpose. The days are shorter and the nights drag along for what seem like extended amounts of time. The darkness is a current reminder of how ridiculously bizarre and upsetting the year has been. I replay the moments unfortunately now with anger built inside for the mistakes allowed. I go through the motions hoping to make it safely to my slumber, moving without a direction and all the while upset with my place in the world's meaning of life.

I wonder, what is it all for, after fighting back a moment of tears which try and infiltrate the mood. I hold back as best as I can, but the memory of the prior life keeps peeking its head into my view. How could I end up in a travel trailer in Biloxi, Mississippi, with not one person around to be my comfort? I am left to think, and the more I allow my mind to square up with my reality, an ugliness brews which I have to ensure doesn't explode.

*****

Last night was hard; temperatures in the low teens, weather I had not even been exposed to in many my better days. I don't have hot water, no heat aside a UV plug-in I am now glad I remembered to bring along as I left in the summer. The silence is deafening, and the loneliness is extremely hard to bear. I lay in bed playing the game Toon Blast as if it was all that I had left while skimming through the television, trying my best to avoid anything that would send me into a mental whirlwind. I eventually get so lost in my head I have to find safety; I lean on my usual in the form of ministry videos provided by YouTube.

The messages as always resonate with my immediate situation and allow me to both look into my own soul while having hope tomorrow would be a better moment as long as I found the strength to not give in, for my situation is mine but doesn't have to be the end of the road. I am only in a tunnel, one such as the same that I poetically spoke on earlier and with all the same passengers. My mental health, I believe, is a testament to what God can provide in the form of a blessing, one that seems to be underappreciated. My mind is a power tool I think has had to endure some of the worst a man could bear this year. I think, wow, I am still sane and able to be reasonable in all my actions as the disease is truly hereditary and runs deep in my family genetic code.

I have had several family members fall prey to its darkness, crime, theft, hallucinations, psychotic episodes, and worst, suicide, yet I am functioning though on my last, in my right frame of thoughts. The issues I once carried about my past still haunt my inside, as now, I am more upset others have ample resources and are able to live life without my pain, but who am I to judge those who walk their walk-in life? I have to focus now on my own journey and find a way to move forward.

Understanding the past is that—it is the past. Days of old I cannot go back and change or rewrite. The issues and obstacles have not harmed my person or placed me into worse, so accepting where I am and understanding the blessing will hopefully allow for healing as I fight to survive.

*****

I have applied for more than fifty jobs and pray that God sees fit my abilities to reacclimate to the world so that I may further my life, so I wait. I have completed several interviews and believe I have more to give to myself and my way of life, so I will await the outcomes as most have returned not hired; I still hold on to hope. I have faith in the process but fear in the journey. I have faith in his power but fear of each uncertain outcome. Celebrated once as an obvious overachiever but decimated to a minute picture of the force I once was. I took down all the pictures of my past and photos of the reminders of my old ways of life hoping that I will be able to create new opportunities to place on my walls.

Living in yesterday is such a negative umbrella at times, when you are on your knees wondering why the visions keep you locked in a mental form of solitary confinement. You lean back on who you were and get upset at who you now are. You find ways to demonize the relationships you once had and find it easy to anger because the parties involved aren't serving the sentence you feel you are right alongside.

I am tired, to say the least, but I am willing. I am tortured, it feels, in my physical form, yet I have continued vision of prosper and a faith which states God sees me and sees my attempts at a better version of the man I was. I have had enough to eat from the pain; I only want to move forward in a better way. One that will allow me to provide better for myself and my pup and give a bit to the world in return for his favor.

I wrote this about love and my lack and learned behavior. I recognize that love is relevant but only a piece to a larger puzzle. Love is big and plays such a unique role, but when you allow yourself to love everything in this material world aside God, well, your life will not be the dream of what you believe love is to provide. It will never amount to the glamour and glitz you see online and in the media. Love cannot create a beautiful picture of rainbows and overflowing blessing. Love is a part of a bigger picture; it is necessary but can never be the only aspect of life you long to live for.

Love provides a way to look at life but should never be the end all, be all, for when you love something or someone more than you love God, well, you will end up like myself. Longing to be loved and alone relearning the basic avenues of life.

You will be left to reanalyze life's decisions and play back all the ugliness which led you to darkness. You will have time to find blame and place fault all while still sitting in the stink of what you were chasing. You will hope you can salvage pieces of your life, searching for empathy from the Creator and listening to the voices in your head which all claim to have the way forward.

It's Christmas, and I feel I have nothing to celebrate when in all actuality I have life. I have a newfound spirit and think the past was a gift to learn how to live upright and just. I have been given a newfound unique set of skills, and they are more powerful than any I have previously assumed I acquired. I can be who I want as long as I continue to believe that God has my best interest and favor in his hands. I pray as I can and cry as needed to show I am in agreeance with his ways. I repent for my past and thank him for the same.

I won't have the same celebrated holidays as many. I will not be opening gifts and around those I love. I know this holiday, and those moving forward I am with God, and I hope I can keep this open frame of mind as the years pass. It is hard enough to be in the midst of society and all the evil which is currently taking our world by storm. The mass shootings and daily killings, the plagues and natural disasters which disrupt so many different elements of life. The continued hatred and unloving ways amongst all people. The cold shoulders and blind eyes displayed daily. Is this America? Is this the new world? Is this love? If so, I guess maybe where I currently sit is best as I am not the vision of ugliness displayed in the current state of affairs. I am simply a man, one who lives in sin yet fully believes in a better way of life with or without you. But God, yeah, the God that I now believe is salvaging my spirit and shaking my physical in a way to allow for me to enlighten many. Yeah, I will dance and scream His praise as long as I am allowed to be a part of whatever He has planned.

I know, I know; it is easier said than done and a challenge moving forward. There will be many more lonely nights and darkened days, I am sure, but at least I know my heart, and if I can at least put one foot forward day by day, maybe, just maybe, there is a chance I can allow God to wash my back of the dirt and damage I carry center of my back.

As we move into the New Year, I ask that we all find a way to better present ourselves moving forward. Peace amongst society. Is that really too much to ask for? The balance of life is moving toward an end. What will holidays mean if there's nothing to celebrate as the days move forward? When will things shift to better way of life? If you are doing great and your neighbor suffers, are you really doing what you are supposed to do with the blessings you have acquired?

Take nothing for granted. Believe me. I know that as fast as it was given, it may all be taken away.

You may be forced to relive the possibilities you had to create a legacy which involved humanitarian efforts and paying it forward. There are too many individuals living in worse standards than myself. This makes me wonder how much is enough, especially to those who have extreme amounts of blessings and unlimited resources. What would it take for unity? How hard is it to place humankind above your list of popularity and social acceptance? Well, until this can be answered, we will forever live in a society that sees "I" as more important than "us," and a place where "me" will be held higher than "we."

I can only pray that as we move into a new year, I can find a focus to allow me to be the pillar which creates a change not only for myself but for several others. A chance to change my life and many others along the way. This isn't me trying to be life's savior but me trying to follow out the original blueprint or all mankind. To simply create a place where we all can coexist amongst the original beauty we were gifted to be in amongst other unique and beautiful beings.

Life in God's original blueprint for humanity, one that is built on love.

Is your heart bigger than your head? I listen to Pastor Jakes ask, as I wrestle with my sanity. I believe so, I reply.

He yells out, "Love will never fail. Love will always prevail!"

And now I have a full understanding as to what love is to be in the life. I hope and pray God will allow me to live.

A love in which material and acceptance no longer play a major part. The luxurious things I once pursued are mere remnants of the peace I so hope to acquire as I move forward. To remove myself from fear and anger at my past to make room for a heart to be filled with emotions which travel through each and every part of my being. Turning my past and hatred into platforms I can use to ensure others will soon look at and see as a blueprint for a way forward to be able to scream from the mountaintops, "Nevertheless, I live!"

There are so many people I need to ultimately thank for the undying support this past year. The intense amount of pain, trials, and tribulations were a direct reflection of life choices from my past in which I personally allowed to overtake my way of thinking.

Influenced by popular culture and socialization, it was very easy to slip into a state of mind which would allow for me to feel less than even though I knew for a fact my strength was far more intense than my doubts. The forces of the outside were pulling at my weakest parts totally engulfing my nurturing spirit and forcing me to dislike life.

I love all and thank each and every person who has provided me with insight along this journey. Whether you were a direct or indirect influence, your powerful prayers, support, and place in my heart and journey will forever be irreplaceable.

God, I truly regret the way I avoided the level of love and support you have for me. I apologize for my ignorance and ask that you will find it worthy to increase upon me spiritual understanding and favor as the days continue to press forward. I am a man who is in the midst of a storm that I know only you have been able to afford me opportunity to reach higher ground. I have seen highs and extreme lows in this life, and with your direction, I now know that I can move forward with a head held high. I understand my life was not my own; it was a gift, and I took advantage of the gift given to me. I ask that you continue to work on my spirit. Please, God, ensure that I can hold up to the standard of life you set forth for me.

To my parents, life has never been the picture of perfect, and there have been so many storms placed in our way. The gift, I believe, was the fact we are still alive to have the conversations about the rights and the wrongs. I only in life wanted to be a child in which you were proud to say was your own. I have made many mistakes, and I apologize for any and all adversity I brought to your doorstep and hope that we can move forward in life as a unit regardless the prior obstacles. Forever I love you both.

To my sister, we are not perfect and have many issues amongst us as we didn't have choice to be family. I hope that one day we are able to be who we once were and laugh amongst each other and able to watch our children grown old. We only have the opportunity to live this life once, so if it is in God's plan one day, we will meet in better spirits to enjoy life as family should.

To my extended blood relatives, I forgive you all for the absence I have harbored as a reason to be angry and upset. For the good and, more important, the bad memories, I release and let it all go, for it needs to be in God's hand to work out as I will refrain from being bitter. I pray we all are blessed in His name and able to find a common ground to ensure our ancestry is memorable and one that sounds of promise and purpose.

To my ex-wife Leigh and my sons, LeRon Junior and LeRon III. I own each and every aspect of the way our life has tailed in respect to my actions. I never wanted things to go as they went, but I was young and not man enough to stop being the virus which infected a household I created. I refrain from continuing to blame your mother for what she wouldn't and couldn't do as I had options, and no one made me stay and live the life I did. I own my sins and am sorry I have created a wedge in our home which continues to drive us apart to this day. Leigh, everything you have gotten from me you earned, so I no longer harbor hate about my situation and what I have to pay or let go as for my responsibilities. To my boys, I want you to know I am proud of you and only wish that we could create a bond that will ensure you both have the opportunity to be the men in this life your father couldn't be. I love you all.

Lakeisha, I thank you for the opportunity to find myself in life and love. For the first time I had the chance to do it my way, and even though you gave me an opportunity to have love and the life I longed for, I carried the ugliness of my past with me. I lost the one person I truly loved and rightfully so as I couldn't let my ignorant ways go, to simply believe you were in it with me and not alone for yourself. I do not know if it was you or if we were to be, but in my heart, I know it was right and where I should have been. I pray life continues to bless you and you find all the love and support I withheld as we have one life, and I plan to be your biggest cheerleader as long as I can. Thank you for everything you afforded me and all you did to support my efforts. I will forever love you. I now know I can never allow myself to love a woman more than I love God, which is what I allowed myself to do.

Sharee Smith, I appreciate your support and hand on getting me moving forward with this writing, as if you had not placed the seed in my head, I would have never placed a pen in my hand. You have given me a spiritual base that was lost. You gave me a chance to find my soul again. The ability to know that you can have a friendship which is not based around alcohol, sex, and weed smoke. One that can have a root based on the Lord and our way of life.

New Covenant, you are amazing, and each and every time I am ever in McDonough, Georgia, I plan on ensuring I am in attendance to receive the word of God. The fellowship you afford is like no other. Please keep saving souls and sending them to the Father, one by one.

Tiffany Ross and Mervetta Shaw, thank you for continuing to check on me and my stubborn ways. I appreciate your ears and eyes as you read and reread my work to assist me in making sure I had a product good enough to share with the world. It means a lot to know I have and always had ones in my corner who genuinely wanted to see me succeed. Your genuine support is noteworthy and does not go overlooked.

Bicentennial Church, Redstone, Arsenal, you were pivotal in my early stages of transition. I was down and in a very weak and altered mind state. You offered your services and placed me ten toes up and in the right direction as I was searching for the answers to my emotions. The unity you displayed and the chance to be in the word was a high moment of my turning point. I was desperate, and you never turned your hand. Thank you for all you did to place me on track.

To each RV park (Redstone RV Park, Scott AFB RV Park, Millington RV Park, NAS Jacksonville RV Park, NAS Pensacola Blue Angel RV Park, Keesler AFB RV Park), thank you. This was a new experience, and it was challenging to be alone and deal with my struggles day in and day out. You each provided a service and worked with my issues in travel never leaving me without. Thank you to all.

About the Author

LeRon was born in Milwaukee, Wisconsin, and raised in St. Louis, Missouri, where the script of his life began. As the oldest of two, he found many mischievous means to occupy his time. His life has been one for the storybooks literally, having had many struggles throughout, yet they all have allowed for him to have a testimony in which he has begun sharing with the world.

As a retired naval veteran of twenty-six years, he has completed an AAS in Electronics, a BA in Psychology, and a BS in Business Administration. He has deployed twelve times and retired honorably as a Senior Chief Petty Officer. After the dust cleared and civilian life kicked in, he found himself searching for who he truly was. The deep hole in his heart was self-inflicted, and it was bandaged by means of several worldly crutches which hindered his growth in life. There was a void in him which was a direct reflection of not having an ongoing relationship with God throughout most of his adulthood though he accepted Christ at a young age.

This void led to several bad decisions and his open acceptance to allow Christ to use him as a tool to tell a story which many may feel parallels their own struggles in finding themselves with respect to their faith, family, career, and love. He loves to spend time with his best friend, a four-year-old Yorkshire terrier named Ratchet, exercising, creating music, and continually trying to follow the narrow path best he can.

Printed in the USA
CPSIA information can be obtained
at www.ICGtesting.com
CBHW030900201124
17650CB00026B/626